State Schools since the 1950s:
the good news

Adrian Elliott

Trentham Books

Stoke on Trent, UK and Sterling, USA

Trentham Books Limited
Westview House   22883 Quicksilver Drive
734 London Road   Sterling
Oakhill   VA 20166-2012
Stoke on Trent   USA
Staffordshire
England ST4 5NP

First published 2007

British Library Cataloguing-in-Publication Data
A catalogue record for this book is available from the British Library

ISBN: 978 1 85856 372 5

Designed and typeset by Trentham Print Design Ltd, Chester, and
printed in Great Britain by cpod, Wiltshire.

Contents

Foreword and acknowledgements

This book is the result of my long-standing wish to help put the record straight about the true performance of state schools in this country. Much comment in the media and elsewhere about education is mis-informed, exaggerated or factually incorrect. These views should be challenged. Due to my background the book inevitably concentrates heavily on mainstream secondary education. I have dealt almost exclusively with the situation in England although referring to evidence which treats the United Kingdom as single entity.

I wish to express my gratitude to those without whom the book would not have been possible. First, there are the hundreds of people who responded to my request, in *Saga magazine*, for material on schools in the post-war period. Not all will agree with my conclusions but I deeply appreciate their fascinating, instructive and often moving accounts

I greatly valued the opportunity to discuss the issues raised in the book with Professor Stephen Gorard, of York University and Professor Tim Brighouse, Chief Adviser to London Challenge. I benefited from their wisdom and experience.

I am extremely grateful for the support afforded by the head teachers and staff of the following schools; All Saints, York; Broxholme, Hertfordshire; English Martyrs, York; Holme on Spalding Moor CE primary, East Riding; Kingsmeadow, Gateshead; Maybury primary, Hull; Park High, Harrow and St.Joseph's College, Bradford. But inevitably, any value the book has is also the product of my experience in all the schools I have worked in as well as the hundreds of contacts and friendships created in the process.

I am grateful to the staff of the British Library, John Rylands University of Manchester Library, the National Archives and the University of York Library for their patience and assistance.

Michael Kerrigan, friend, colleague and retired HMI not only proof read the manuscript meticulously but was also a constant source of helpful suggestions and perceptive ideas which invariably led to new and interesting avenues.

I am grateful above all for the support and help offered throughout by my wife and family. Mary's encouragement and unfailingly astute and accurate comments on the work in draft form have made the project possible.

Glossary

BTEC	Business and Technology Education Council (vocational qualification)
DfES	Department for Education and Science
GCE	General Certificate of Education
	A-level Advanced
	O level Ordinary
GCSE	General Certificate of Secondary Education
HMI	Her Majesty's Inspector(s) of Schools
HMCI	Her Majesty's Chief inspector of Schools
JMB	Joint Matriculation Board (now AQA)
KS2	Key stage 2 (7-11 years)
KS3	Key stage 3 (11-14 years)
KS4	Key stage 4 (14-16 years)
LEA (or LA)	Local Education Authority, Local Authority
NA	National Archives
OECD	Organisation for Economic Co-operation and Development
Ofsted	Office for Standards in Education
PISA	Programme for International Student Assessment
PIRLS	Progress in International Reading Literacy
QCA	Qualifications and Curriculum Authority
SEN	Special Educational Needs
TES	*Times Educational Supplement*
TIMSS	Trends in International Maths and Science Survey

1

Is state education failing?

'Ladies and gentlemen, every single one of you in this room...' The speaker, a large man with an impressively deep voice, paused for effect and looked round slowly at his audience, '.... is a total and utter failure in your professional lives'

I don't recall the reaction of others in the room in Oxford, twenty years ago, to the speaker's opening. I remember thinking, as a recently appointed head of a comprehensive school, that it left something to be desired as a motivational technique and I would not be tempted to use it with my new staff. The audience, all secondary head teachers, were then subjected to a wide-ranging attack on state education, particularly those who worked in it. Whilst I thought the odd criticism valid, most were inaccurate or wildly over-stated. The heads, a fairly restrained lot, listened to the attack in polite silence, although towards the end one determined older lady pointed out fiercely that her pupils never used the kind of language with which our speaker, by now well into his stride, was enlivening his talk.

Many years later, now retired, I was flicking through television channels when I came across a trailer for the BBC series, *Grumpy Old Men*. 'Let's face it.' the speaker was saying, '...*all* kids today are illiterate morons'. Shortly after, I heard that Lieutenant-Colonel Tim Collins, whose eve of a battle speech to his troops in Iraq inspired millions, had described state education as a 'basket case'. So whether from the mouths of entrepreneurs, war heroes or comedians, the message had changed little over my twenty years as a head: state schools and those who worked in them were a disaster.

By then our Oxford speaker was long dead, drowned off the Spanish coast after falling from his yacht. Even if Robert Maxwell's many crimes were later exposed, they hardly detracted from the popularity of his views on education. If anything, the portrayal of state education in England by the media, politicians and business leaders has become more negative in the years since his death. Criticisms appear almost daily in books, newspapers, journals and the broadcast media. The specific complaints are familiar enough.

It is said that standards are falling, children are not taught the basics and many are illiterate or enumerate, often both. Too many leave school without qualifications despite the fact that examinations are getting easier by the year. Even university students require remedial lessons before starting their courses. State schools are infected with an all pervading left wing ideology fostered by radical teaching unions, which puts social engineering above academic standards and political correctness above the real needs of children. Heads and teachers abhor any form of competition, above all in sport, which has virtually disappeared from schools as a result. The setting of children by ability is rejected, leading to mediocrity and low standards as teachers teach to the middle ability range and ignore the needs of the brightest and those with special needs. Despite the best efforts of Prince Charles, the classics, particularly Shakespeare, have all but disappeared from schools in favour of studies of the plots of *East Enders* or *Neighbours* and analysis of text messaging. Children's speech has become slovenly and nearly unintelligible. Schools have failed especially with boys, resulting in an ever widening gap in achievement between the sexes.

Behaviour is, inevitably, a favourite target. At best many lessons are disrupted, teachers abused and widespread bullying is tolerated by ineffective, often invisible senior management. At worst state secondary schools are seen, in the words of one speaker at the 2005 Conservative Conference, as 'jungles', violent, intimidating, anarchic places where children and teachers risk serious assault, rape and even murder. In most moral relativism holds sway with staff refusing to condemn or challenge poor behaviour in or outside school.

Many commentators go even further and, when not attacking state education directly, link the failure of schools to wider social and cultural ills, ranging from Britain's lack of success in international sport to growth in crime and anti-social behaviour, the breakdown of family life and economic problems.

Some critics point to a lost golden age in education in the 1950s and early 60s, arguing that grammar schools offered a ladder of opportunity which is now missing for poorer children whilst secondary moderns gave others a good basic education and the practical skills essential for working life. Lastly, our schools are compared unfavourably with those abroad, which are said to achieve higher standards in a calm, ordered atmosphere which is lacking here.

As Peter Wilby, the journalist, remarks

> Teachers have proved ideal scapegoats. They can be blamed for more or less anything: the nation's social, spiritual or physical shortcomings as well as its economic ones. Just as Jews were held responsible for both communism and capitalism, so teachers can be blamed for both upholding the status quo and subverting it. (*Times Educational Supplement*, 28/07/06)

Whilst rejecting these negative views of schools today, I am concerned about the lack of challenge to them. Potential defenders of state education are often so concerned to attack government policies, often with good reason, and agencies such as Ofsted that, like the critics, they leave the overall impression of a service in crisis and on the brink of collapse.

In reality there is considerable evidence suggesting a more optimistic picture of schools today, which refutes both the concept of decline over time and failure in comparison with other countries. In addition, my own experience in no sense reflects the damning views outlined above. I taught for 37 years from 1966 to 2003. Most of my career was spent in northern England, teaching in Catholic schools, including a direct grant grammar school, a primary school and three comprehensives. I spent five years as a deputy head and eighteen as a head. I have also been an Ofsted inspector, acted as an adviser to governors of several schools, mentored new head teachers and helped train and assess potential heads. I met many groups of overseas teachers through links with York University, particularly from Germany and Scandinavia. Earlier, I had taught in Switzerland for three years and have visited schools and universities in several European countries.

Whilst working in Catholic schools might suggest a lack of contact with the most difficult pupils, this was not so. I met many challenging individuals. I have considerably more knowledge and first-hand experience of state schools than most of the media pundits, politicians and industrialists who speak so passionately and confidently about the failings of state education.

Given the polarised nature of educational debate in England today it is also useful to establish where my own views lie. They are neither radical nor unusual amongst secondary head teachers today but no less strongly held. As the ex-head of a church school I place strong emphasis on the moral and spiritual education of children. Schools must have core values based on an acceptance of shared humanity, equality and service to others. As the late Cardinal Basil Hume insisted

> We are not engaged in producing just good performers in the market place or able technocrats. Our task is the training of good human beings, purposeful and wise, themselves with a vision of what it is to be human and the kind of society that makes that possible. (Hansard, House of Lords 05/07/96)

Children achieve infinitely more through encouragement and praise than through punishment and criticism. In the past some schools were content to stress only their social and moral role. Academic achievement and examination success are vital for young people: we still have to produce the 'good performers and technocrats'. Those colleagues who reject school performance statistics whilst claiming they want to concentrate on individual needs are wrong. What are the figures but an aggregate of the achievements of individuals? The problem with performance tables is that too much weight has been given to them. They have too often been used to judge rather than illuminate. As far as teaching methods are concerned, I am a pragmatist. In the hands of inspired practitioners different methods draw amazing responses from children. Whole class teaching, where all the children are actively involved, works well on an individual level: group work does not lead inevitably to mediocrity and disorganisation.

Schools need good order and discipline in order to work. Children should not call staff by their first names. I accept the need for setting whilst recognising that, given the spread of ability in most comprehensive schools, the practice does not remove the need for differentiated teaching. I agree with school uniform and strongly support competitive sport. In short my views are those of the large majority of state secondary school heads in this country.

There are undoubtedly serious problems in state education in this country. Any system with over 20000 schools educating 12.5 million pupils, 93 per cent of the child population, is bound to present at best a mixed picture, with some schools struggling. Many of the problems are long-standing and go back much further than the unfortunate 1960s which are blamed for so many social ills. Differences in achievement between children in schools in this country remain far too great and there are still too many pupils who struggle with basic literacy and numeracy. Low level disruption by some pupils plagues too many classrooms. While the position is improving, too few seventeen year olds are in full-time education compared with the situation in other western countries. The fall in the numbers of pupils taking modern languages to GCSE level and sciences at A-level is another real concern.

Despite such challenges, much criticism of state education today is exaggerated and unfair. A number of errors are common to many critics, such as the tendency to generalise the difficulties of the least successful state schools to all schools when compared with media treatment of the independent system the opposite applies: the academically most successful are portrayed as characteristic of the whole sector. Photographs or film in the media which are intended to represent state and independent sectors side by side also distort the situation.

Even where problems exist their extent is often grossly over-stated. Nobody could over-estimate the damage done to children in a failing school. Tackling this must remain an absolute priority for teachers, government and local authorities. But even within the education service many seem wholly unaware of how atypical such schools are. I conducted a survey of a sample of 100 teachers in both primary and secondary schools who were all working in successful state schools and asked them what percentage of schools they believed were failing Ofsted inspections. They over-estimated, on average, the percentage of failing schools by over four times. Informal straw polls taken amongst friends and relatives who don't work in education suggest that their degree of misconception is even greater.

Where figures are provided, the issue is compounded by gross statistical errors which appear regularly in education stories in the media. One local paper claimed a recent Ofsted report had shown behaviour to be acceptable in only one third of secondary schools. The report *Managing Challenging Behaviour* (2005) stated that behaviour was good or better in 68 per cent of secondary schools, satisfactory in a further 22 per cent and unsatisfactory in 10 per cent – a long way from the two thirds of the story!

The simplest way in which state education is undermined today is the straightforward untruth: the repetition of 'factual' statements for which there is no evidence about what is happening in schools. Where there is considerable counter-evidence this is ignored. Whilst some misinformation, like the 1980s claim that London schools banned the nursery rhyme *Baa, baa, black sheep* as racist, has been laid to rest, other damaging myths, for example about what has been happening to competitive sport in schools, still persist.

The wide coverage given to these allegations arises from the manner in which the media, politicians and others influencing public opinion feed off each other. A politician will quote a newspaper article about the latest 'horror' in state schools. This is then reported by other papers, further disseminating the story. None of this is new but a more recent development is the number of columnists in the press who then pick the story over, re-working it, exaggerating already distorted facts. The final links in this media chain are people who write to local papers or websites claiming confidently that the issue raised applies to every state school in the country. So what began as a single, wholly untypical incident in one school ends up being viewed as a daily occurrence in every classroom in the land!

I examine several areas where I believe people have been misled about the true state of education today. The first is through an exaggerated view of the success of schools in this country in the past and the standards achieved in them. Clearly, in any activity, economic, social, scientific, or artistic, overstating the achievements of the past can reflect badly on the present. In this country we are particularly prone to view the past with a benevolent nostalgia and whilst not all critics of modern schools believe in a post-war educational golden age, many certainly do.

Secondly there are the claims made of the alleged failings of schools in England compared with those abroad. Whilst accurate international comparisons are notoriously difficult to make, there is a wealth of evidence both from international testing and the views of educationalists from other countries that the image presented of our schools lurking in the relegation zone of some vast world-wide league table is incorrect.

The crucial area of standards in schools today is considered. Abundant proof exists, despite views to the contrary, of genuine, sustained improvement in the academic achievement of children across all ability levels and from all backgrounds. Our children have never been better taught at any time. Acceptance of the need to eradicate areas of under-achievement, particularly amongst the poorest in society, does not justify either denigrating the outstanding efforts of those working in socially disadvantaged areas or pretending that under-achievement is more widespread than it is. Too many who write and speak about education do both.

Of great concern is the issue of our children's behaviour, attitudes and moral, development. Many commentators link the supposed failings of schools in this area with national anxiety about a perceived moral malaise and spiritual vacuum. As with academic standards, there is a strong emphasis by many on alleged deterioration over time. This view, too, is simplistic and over-pessimistic.

In this country we have always rightly regarded extra-curricular activities, especially in sport, music and drama, as an essential part of school life. Much has been said and written over recent years about their decline and even total disappearance, especially in the case of sport. This is often attributed to ideology, an argument as false as the view of what has actually happened in schools.

Finally, the work of several schools is described. These are typical of many state schools today and are as effective as any in the western world.

2

Selective education:
a truly golden age?

In the autumn of 1965 I entered a school, Erith Grammar School in Kent, for the first time as a trainee teacher. At the first break time, three of us were approached by the deputy head and asked to leave the staff room. My heart sank. The school had seemed welcoming and friendly, not the type of institution where student teachers were expected to take their breaks in airless stock rooms. We were pleased to discover that the request had nothing to do with our status: an emergency staff meeting had been called because the school had just heard it was to become comprehensive. The teachers were angry and confused, especially as it was likely that the new school would be established across two sites.

From my first day in a school in a professional capacity forty years ago through to my retirement and beyond, the debate over selective versus comprehensive education has never disappeared. Just when the arguments appeared to have been settled they have re-surfaced: like some dreadful Sicilian blood feud the issue never seems to die. In 1997 the Tories under John Major went to the country with a policy of a grammar school in every town.

More recently the debate has been re-ignited by a report in 2005 from the London School of Economics which was commissioned by the Sutton Trust, an organisation whose laudable aim is to improve access to higher education for the poorest children. The report claimed that British society has become less equal since the late 1950s (Blanden *et al*, 2005). A number of commentators blamed this on the abolition of grammar schools and the call for the return of selection which followed came not only from the political right. Nick Cohen, writing in the *Observer* under the headline 'Long live grammar schools', claimed that 'this is a more class-ridden country than when the grammar schools were in place' (31/07/05). *The Sunday Times* argued on similar lines that ' the abolition of most grammar schools kicked away the ladder for children from poorer backgrounds'(28/08/05).

Clearly the LSE report and its reception in the press offered a serious challenge to those who argue that grammar schools did not achieve the levels of social mobility claimed for them and that comprehensive schools have not been the social and educational disaster which opponents maintain. The LSE team looked at two cohorts of boys born in 1958 and 1970 respectively. It divided the group up into quartiles based on their parents' income and did so again based on their own income when they reached their early thirties in 1991 and 2000 respectively. It discovered that mobility between the quartiles was less for those born in 1970 than for those born in 1958. The chances of a child born to the poorest parents remaining poor had increased from 1958 to 1970 as had the chances of those born to the richest households staying rich. It was also claimed that the situation in Britain was unique, in marked contrast to Germany, Canada and Denmark, Finland, Norway and Sweden. In all these countries social mobility across income groups increased. The United States had the least mobility after Britain but it had stayed the same: only in Britain had the position worsened.

The report suggested that the key issue in low social mobility was education. Whilst the educational attainment levels of all the income groups had risen over the period, the increase had been significantly less for those from the poorest backgrounds. In particular, staying-on rates at school after 16 and the achievement of higher education qualifications had risen much more amongst wealthier children than amongst the poor. Much of the press coverage on the report stressed the disappearance of grammar schools as a key factor in the apparent reduction in the life chances of the poor. Tim Luckhurst in the *Times* even argued that 'only a blend of ideological zeal and intellectual dishonesty' could now defend the comprehensive system (09/08/05).

However, serious questions exist about both the study and its interpretation by the media. Professor Stephen Gorard and Dr.Emma Smith of York University have expressed reservations about the methodology of the research (Gorard and Smith, 2005). Further, the report says that only 35 per cent of the shift in inter-generational mobility was due to educational factors: this is significant but was not reflected in most media coverage, which implied that education was the sole cause. An even more crucial issue which was totally ignored by commentators, who used the report to attack comprehensive schools, is that the five countries which have the highest levels of social mobility, the Nordic nations and Canada, all have well-established comprehensive systems of education.

The data only dealt with boys. Had information about girls been available it might have confirmed the existing findings but there is evidence that girls from poor backgrounds have benefited significantly more than poor boys from increased educational opportunities over the same period. Also a greater proportion of children in the sample from 1970 would have been born to ethnic minority families than in the 1958 group. Social mobility amongst ethnic groups is low and many families remain in the poorest income groups. Whilst the report refers to race and ethnicity as a factor in the static social mobility of the USA, no such link is made in the UK .

Working-class boys born in 1970 and leaving school at 16 also entered a very different job market from those born in 1958. The number of jobs in manufacturing, in shipbuilding, steel making or mining had fallen. These occupations offered opportunities for less academic boys to gain promotion to supervisory, managerial or union posts. The later cohort, even if better educated, entered an employment market where prospects were more dependent on educational qualifications and social skills.

Above all, two misconceptions completely undermine the interpretation put on the report by writers such as Cohen and Luckhurst. First, the entire basis of their interpretation of the report, that children born in 1958 were educated within a selective system and those in 1970 in a comprehensive system, is incorrect.

Writers, mistakenly, concentrated only on the birth dates of the two groups. But the key period was when they were at secondary school and especially, because of the importance attached to staying on at school, the end of their compulsory time at school at 16. Children from poor families, in particular, often decide whether to stay on at school quite late. The 1958 cohort were not 16 until 1974: by then 70 per cent of children were already in comprehensive schools. The assumption, made by nearly every newspaper covering the Sutton report, that the 1958 children were overwhelmingly the products of the selective school age, is wrong. In fact grammar and secondary modern schools had already disappeared in large areas of the country, particularly in the north and midlands where many less well-off families lived.

But if the false interpretation of the report rests on one fallacy, it also rests on a more common, long-standing myth. This is the belief that large numbers of the poorest children succeeded in grammar schools whereas their modern counterparts are failing in the comprehensive system. This view is gaining more credence as time passes, often disseminated by those too young to have experienced a country-wide selective system.

In the late 1970s, whilst in Cambridge on a teacher fellowship, someone expressed surprise to me that, living in Bradford, I was in favour of comprehensive education. 'After all', he said, 'the grammar school system in your area has benefited so many famous children from working class families'. I asked for examples and he mentioned Harold Wilson, Barbara Castle and Denis Healey. He believed, like many, that grammar school children who came from northern cities, such as Bradford and spoke with an identifiable accent, must all have been working-class. In fact Barbara Castle's father was a tax inspector who curbed 'his passion for foreign trips and continental wine' to send her as a fee-payer to Bradford Girls' Grammar School. Denis Healey's father was the principal of Keighley Technical College, whose modern equivalents earn six-figure salaries, whilst James Wilson, father of Harold, was an industrial chemist. None were remotely working-class. All were educated before the era under discussion but the truth was still more complex than my Cambridge colleague appreciated.

There were children from working class backgrounds who reached grammar schools, benefited hugely from the opportunities there and went on to lead successful and rewarding lives: it would be foolish to suggest otherwise. But working-class children in the 50s accounted for three-quarters of all children whereas today they are barely a third. Any comparison of achievement over time must take account of this difference. Grammar schools then could not have survived without working-class pupils. Even in the 50s, the proportion of all working class children in grammar schools was low in relation to their total numbers in society. What is more significant, in light of the renewed argument over comprehensive education, is the fact that the number of the poorest children in grammar schools, those from the unskilled and semi-skilled working-class, the unemployed or those in care, was extremely small compared with the better off working-class.

Children who fail in comprehensive schools today generally come from families where home circumstances hinder academic progress. This is not to deny that there are some schools which are so bad that it is difficult for any child to succeed, nor is it meant to blame the families whose children struggle at school. But children are failing, and not just in England, from families where there is extreme poverty, lack of parental educational achievement or interest in school, severe illness, other family trauma or severe cultural or linguistic obstacles. These factors are familiar to everyone in education.

Whilst children from the better off and better educated working-class were selected for grammar school, albeit in relatively small numbers, the proportion of children from families with problems which today would make them most at risk of failing in comprehensive schools was minuscule. The academic performance of various social groups in the selective system is considered later.

The 1944 Education Act institutionalised secondary education for all. It did not, as often believed, create the tri-partite system of grammar, technical and secondary modern schools. Both the Spens Report of 1938 and the Norwood Report, five years later, proposed such a system and most LEAs supported the proposals, on grammar and secondary modern schools at least. About one in six grammar schools were direct grant, supported by central, not local, funding, still partly fee paying and normally more prestigious and selective than local authority grammar schools. Technical schools never provided for more than 4 per cent of the population whilst in the immediate post-war period, authorities such as the London County Council and Swansea were already expressing interest in comprehensive education. The first such school was opened on Anglesey in 1947.

During the heyday of the selective system in the late 1950s, under 30 per cent of children attended grammar schools, including direct grant grammar schools, 62 per cent secondary moderns and the rest technical, comprehensive and bi-lateral schools which were nominally comprehensive but with rigidly separated grammar and secondary modern sections. As children on average stayed longer in grammar school the actual number entering these schools was far fewer than 30 per cent: the figure in England, alone, was around 20 per cent. The proportion of children admitted to grammar schools also varied widely across different parts of the country, ranging from less than 10 per cent in Gateshead and Sunderland to over 40 per cent in Westmoreland. (McKibbin, 1998 p227)

Fear that the new system would not benefit poorer children as much as had been hoped was evident from the earliest days. The Labour Party Conference in 1947 passed a resolution, deploring a situation which resulted in

> ...children from well-to-do homes being educated together whilst the abler children in working-class families are separated from their less gifted brothers and sisters. (Jones, 2003 p29)

But this prompts the question of how many of those abler children from working-class families actually attended the new-style grammar schools.

The answer depended very much on which section of the working class you belonged to. The registrar-general divided the population into six social classes according to the occupation of the head of household. They were: higher professional, lower professional, clerical, skilled manual, semi-skilled manual and unskilled manual – more familiar as classes A, B, CI, CII, D and E. Following the 1951 census the percentages of these groups across the entire country were as follows:

Table 1: Distribution of social classes: 1951 census

Professional:	A 3 per cent
Managerial:	B 15 per cent } 26 per cent
Clerical:	CI 8 per cent
Skilled working	CII 45 per cent
Semi -skilled working	D 16 per cent } 74 per cent
Unskilled/unemployed	E 13 per cent

Only a quarter of the population was upper or middle-class and three-quarters was working-class. It is widely known that social classes A and B and CI were over-represented in grammar schools and that social classes CII, D and E were under-represented. Indeed local studies in Huddersfield (Jackson and Marsden, 1966 p25), and in the north-west, Middlesbrough and Hert-fordshire (Lacey, 1970 p28/29) suggest that the proportion of poorer children in grammar schools, although not their total numbers, may actually have been lower in the 1950s than before, even less than before the war.

What is not always understood was the gap which existed in the proportions of children going to grammar schools within the working class. In 1966, Brian Jackson and Denis Marsden published their study of the experiences of working-class grammar school pupils in Huddersfield. Their research sug-gested that a child from social class B (lower professional) was about 4.5 times more likely to complete a full seven-year grammar school course than a child from a CII (skilled manual) background. The same child, however, from the CII family was, him or herself, 3.5 times more likely to complete grammar school than a child from social class E (Jackson and Marsden, 1966 p23). The educational gap between children from different sections of the working class was almost as great as that between the upper working-class child and one from the middle range of the middle class.

Jackson and Marsden's data involved completion rates at grammar school which were likely to have been influenced by economic circumstances, but another study by Zweig (1961) showed a similar pattern, even for admission to grammar school at eleven. Zweig looked at the lives of industrial workers in Sheffield, Workington, Luton, Birmingham and Mitcham. In the families surveyed only about 14 per cent of children of secondary school age were at grammar schools. This seems a plausible figure, given the bias in grammar school places towards the middle class. But a breakdown of the figures within the different groups of workers reveals a surprising picture. Whilst nearly 25 per cent of the children of supervisory and skilled workers had passed the 11+, the figure for semi- and unskilled workers was under 8 per cent. As Zweig does not separate the semi-skilled figures from the unskilled, it could be assumed, given the trend of his statistics and those of Jackson and Marsden, that the percentage of children from unskilled working-class families in his sample who were going to grammar school would be tiny. Two sociologists from Nottingham University, undertaking research in a deprived part of the city, found that

> when we took a count of the number of children who obtained grammar school places from St.Ann's, it was so small that we could not believe our own results... we found they were 1.5 per cent of the school population. (Coates and Silburn, 1970 p136)

Yet the results were later confirmed through the city education department. Figures from the Crowther report (p133), based on a survey of thousands of national service recruits, also showed that fewer than 10 per cent of the poorest quarter of the population went to grammar school. And Lacey cites a large primary school in a poor area of the north-west where only three children out of 160 passed the 11+ in four years during the 1960s (Lacey, 1970 p35)

Jackson and Marsden identified many of the families of working-class children who went to Huddersfield grammar schools as 'sunken middle class' (pp 67-70). These were families which had, for example, formerly owned their own businesses or who had close relatives in middle-class occupations. Some fathers were foremen or held other supervisory posts, several in charge of as many as fifty workers. In some families parents themselves had attended grammar schools whilst others were office holders in local churches, political parties, unions or music groups. Examples abound of successful children from families with high aspirations where the divide between the middle and working class was blurred. Lorna Sage, the late writer and academic, appears at first glance to be the product of a typical working-class home. She was the daughter of a coal haulier, brought up in a council house, who passed the 11+

and went on to university. But the family also had strong middle-class connections. Her grandfather was a vicar and her father ended the war as an
army captain (Sage, 2000).

Sir Rhodes Boyson, Conservative M.P, junior minister under Mrs.Thatcher
and earlier a headteacher, was regarded as the epitome of the working-class
boy from a Lancashire mill town who rose as a result of grammar schooling.
But his father was also a full-time union official, councillor and chairman of
the local Labour party. Unusually for the area, he brought his own house for
over £600 and was even the chairman of governors of the grammar school
attended by his son. Rhode's mother was a pillar of the local Methodist church
who taught in Sunday school (Boyson, 1995).

Those who exaggerate the opportunities offered by the selective system to
poor children often over-simplify the class structure in industrial regions,
viewing working-class areas as far more homogeneous than they really were.
Sometimes a child gaining a place at grammar school was a sign of the
success of an already upwardly mobile working-class family. My grandfather,
born in 1860, appears in the 1901 census as a miner living in a poor cottage in
Whitwood, Yorkshire. My father, born in 1906, attended Normanton grammar
school and later St.Mark's College, Chelsea. Yet even before my father had left
primary school my grandfather had secured a managerial post at the colliery
and moved to a pleasant terrace house with a bathroom and inside lavatory,
where my grandmother lived comfortably until her death at nearly 100.

But if the poorest working-class families were so under-represented, it could
be argued that the distribution of grammar and secondary modern school
places, at the time, reflected the spread of ability across the social classes. Did
middle-class children achieve more grammar school places simply because
they were brighter? Did most working-class children fail the 11+ because they
were academically weaker than their peers? This was not the case. In 1964, the
results of NFER tests, taken by over 3000 11 year-olds in the late 50s, were
analysed by J.W.B. Douglas (1964 p180). The children had taken tests with a
standard mean of 50 in verbal and non-verbal reasoning, arithmetic, reading
and vocabulary. Douglas then correlated the test results against the type of
secondary school attended. He demonstrated convincingly that there was a
bias in the system in favour of middle-class children which was not
accounted for by ability. Even at the higher levels of the test where pupils had
scored over 60, middle-class children had a significantly better chance of
achieving a grammar school place than their working-class counterparts. The
difference was most marked amongst borderline grammar school entrants. A

pupil who scored between 52 and 54 in the test was *four* times more likely to be at a grammar school if he or she was from a middle-class family, than if they came from the unskilled working-class: an enormous difference for the same score.

The possibility remains that working-class parents preferred to send their children to secondary modern schools and declined grammar school places. Financial constraints certainly affected some families. Irene Smith of Criccieth writes of how one girl in her class deliberately cheated during the 11+ examination and told the teacher, 'My dad told me to cheat because he couldn't afford the uniform' (*Saga magazine*, 01/05 p42). Stephanie Lowe's mother had to turn down a grammar school place in Blackpool because she could not afford the uniform and a number of children in the top stream of the secondary modern which Stephanie attended were in a similar position. The cost of fares, and concern that the child would not be contributing to the family income until the age of 16 or later would also have deterred some families. Nerves, even desperation, may have affected some if they had been prepared as sensitively for the 11+ as the fictional Duncan Thaw, living in Glasgow, in Alasdair Gray's novel *Lanark*:

> One day Mr. Thaw said... 'You realise how important this exam is? If you pass you'll go to a senior secondary school... take your Higher Leaving Certificate and work at anything you like. If you fail... you'll have to take any job you can get'... Mr. Thaw patted his son's back 'Go to it!' he said.
>
> Thaw went to his bedroom, shut the door and lay on the bed and started crying. The future his father indicated seemed absolutely repulsive
>
> (Gray, 1981 p147).

The writer Ferdinand Mount goes further than finance or nerves, claiming that the traditional and basic methods of the secondary modern schools appealed to many working-class parents and that it was only middle-class educationalists who 'mocked' the secondary moderns (Mount, 2004 p272). It is true that many children settled happily into secondary modern schools, as will be shown in chapter 3. However it is not the case that most working-class parents accepted this option with any enthusiasm. Martin analysed parents' preferences for secondary schools in the mid-50s (Martin in Glass, 1954). Predictably, less than 2 per cent of professional and managerial parents wanted their child to attend a secondary modern school whilst over 80 per cent preferred a grammar or technical grammar school. But even amongst the poorest parents, the unskilled working class, only 24 per cent sought a secondary modern education for their child compared with over 60 per cent who aspired, unsuccessfully in most cases, to grammar or technical grammar schools. As early as 1947 the *Daily Mirror* reported that parents in the mining village of Hucknall in Nottinghamshire were complaining to the councillors about an anti-working class bias in the 11+ (10/07/47).

These views are explained, perhaps, by the comment of one teachers' union leader that, 'it was difficult to sell the secondary modern school to parents because it did not seem to lead anywhere' (Jones, 2003 p30). The journalist, Peter Laurie, surely exaggerated when he wrote in 1965 that 'to have been consigned to the limbo of the secondary modern is to have failed disastrously, and very early in life' (Sandbrook, 2005 p422) but it must have felt close to that for some children. Nor would parents have been reassured by contemporary newspaper headlines:

> 'Teachers would 'keep own children from these schools' *Nottingham Guardian*, April 1953.

> 'Is your child 'doomed' at a Modern school?' *Portsmouth Evening News*, August 1953.

> 'Send my child to a town school? No, never!' *Doncaster Gazette*, May 1956

> (Taylor, 1963 pp164-9).

It is clear that many working-class and poor children whose parents wanted them to attend grammar schools and who were bright enough to have taken full advantage of the teaching did not end up there. There is no evidence that children in the 1950s and early 60s with similar social characteristics to those most likely to fail academically in secondary schools today, were awarded grammar school places in any significant numbers. The clamour in some sections of the press that a return to selection would benefit the poorest is based on ignorance of the past. If the return of grammar schools would benefit the poor so greatly, why are only 3 per cent of children in the remaining 160 or so state grammar schools eligible for free school meals – less than a quarter of the national average?

3

Secondary schools in the 1950s

The next three chapters examine the experience of children at school in the 1950s and early 60s, the quality of teaching, the curriculum and the outcomes in terms of examination results. I looked at over 300 inspection reports on schools written by Her Majesty's Inspectors (HMI), mostly between 1955 and 1961. Readers of *Saga magazine* sent over 280 letters and e-mails about state school life in the 50s and 60s in response to my appeal for information. Many wrote lengthy, often moving, accounts of their experiences and these are the source of most of the original comments which appear below. The *Saga* respondents divided as follows:

Gender: 62% female
                                        38% male

School attended: 53% secondary modern
                                  38% grammar or technical grammar school
                                    6% comprehensive or bilateral
                                    2% unclear

As well as the obvious gender bias, grammar schools were over-represented and secondary modern schools under-represented in the sample. It quickly became clear that a disproportionate number of secondary modern respondents had been in the top streams of their schools, which meant that respondents were overwhelmingly from the top half of the ability range. Where possible the emphasis was on 1955 onwards for two reasons: it covers the time when I was at secondary school, and the period immediately after the war involved too many deep-rooted problems in the educational system to make any comparison with the present day fair or meaningful.

In writing a balanced account of the latter part of the period and in trying to determine the extent to which this was, as Lord Tebbit and others would have us believe, an educational golden age, it would be perverse not to recognise the huge obstacles facing schools. By the end of the war school building stock was in a dreadful state. Virtually no re-building or major repair work had taken place in six years and up to a fifth of schools had been damaged by bombing. Financial problems after the war further delayed any effective replacement programme or updating of equipment, which crippled subjects like science. Above all, schools suffered from staff shortages. The raising of the school leaving age in 1947 to 15 increased the total school population by over 10 per cent at a stroke. Added to the post-war population bulge this meant that by the early 50s an under-trained teaching force was facing huge classes in crumbling, sometimes dangerous buildings.

By the second part of the decade spending was increasing on education and improvements to the infrastructure were apparent. Between the world war and the early 60s the percentage of the national income devoted to education doubled and the teaching force increased by seventy per cent.

Expectations were rising as fast. For all the horrendous difficulties created by the two world wars and the depression in the forty years before 1955, most people were aware that the creation of a public education system fit for the twentieth century was desperately overdue. As early as 1926, the Hadow Report had recommended the raising of the school leaving age to 15. It should have happened on September 1st 1939 when the war intervened. When the post-war Labour government finally brought this about in 1947 a rider was added to the act stating that it should be further raised to 16 'as soon as practicably possible'. This did not happen for 26 years and despite the best intentions of R.A. Butler and the 1944 Act many secondary-age children continued to receive what was effectively a primary education in buildings unsuitable for teenagers.

Novelist Angela Carter underlined this sense of opportunities too long denied when writing about the 'select' children from working-class backgrounds who went to grammar school. 'And were they grateful? Were they hell!' (Jones, 2003 p59).

Other children, including many of my *Saga* contacts, did feel grateful for the increased opportunities provided by the 1944 Act. Pat Clayton, daughter of a car-park attendant, went to a grammar school in the north-east and although she had mixed feelings about the way she was treated there, she still feels she owes her success to the excellent education she received. Dr. Hazel Russman from London was also grateful for a 'good education for all children who proved intelligent enough to benefit from it.' Marian Margan from Wales felt she and her friends were 'fortunate to have been educated in a period when standards were high and teachers were allowed to teach'.

Nor are such positive views restricted to ex-grammar school pupils. Many correspondents clearly valued their time at secondary modern and technical schools. Rosemary Nash believed her school was very good and enjoyed her years there. Anne Jordan related how, when she applied for a post with the NHS in Worcestershire, the manager explained that he preferred girls from the local secondary school to those from the grammar school because they were 'better grounded'. Interestingly, some people, like Ted Marsh from London or Joan Hodgson from North Yorkshire, felt they had benefited from not going to a grammar school. In Joan's case, she was able to make a direct comparison as she went to a grammar school sixth form after five years in a secondary school. She found the girls in her new school immature and the regulations petty, including the insistence on sixth form girls wearing berets. Others, like Brenda Morrison from South London, benefited from a second chance, attending a technical school from the second year where she felt 'so proud to wear the blazer.. and to be part of the whole college concept, it was a magical time'.

Teaching and the curriculum are discussed later but other positive aspects of school life which correspondents mentioned were the leadership of some heads, discipline and behaviour, extra-curricular activities and the support of individual teachers. As ever, they considered the best head teachers to have been men and women of vision and humanity, dedicated to learning. Dr Ian Keil remembers his head at a Wiltshire grammar as a 'caring, honest and thoughtful man... whose support for a rather diffident boy was uncondi-tional'. Ian kept in touch with him for over 50 years until his death at the age of 90. Christine Jackson recalls her headmistress in Oxfordshire as 'a person of considerable patience and insight,' fighting the belief that 'as girls only get married, why waste public money educating them?' Sadly, she often lost her battles and the 'old prejudices came to the fore again and many able and bright girls were forced to leave school by parents reluctant to see that times were changing'. David King, a pupil at a mixed grammar in Middlesex, was impressed by the degree of democracy instigated by his headteacher, which was unusual in a 50s school, with pupils even voting on uniform, 'a very hot issue with girls, especially when the 'New Look' came in'.

They remarked on the good discipline and behaviour in schools at the time, often making unfavourable comparisons with the present. Like Sylvia Hilton in Middlesbrough, many felt discipline was fair, whilst Rob Vosey said that corporal punishment was used sparingly for 'crimes like bullying'. Phillip Crosland, at a secondary modern in the East Riding of Yorkshire, was never aware of punishment being used unjustly and again stressed that corporal punishment was used only occasionally. Most correspondents supported it when used appropriately. Several also mentioned that uniform regulations were strictly enforced, although the Newsom Report commented on the 'considerable difficulty' many secondary modern schools found in getting older pupils to wear the correct uniform (Newsom, 1963 p232).

Some correspondents wrote enthusiastically about extra-curricular activities, although a few mistakenly believed that they have disappeared from schools today. Jim Lee told of his London secondary modern school organising trips to Paris, 'where we couldn't believe all the goodies available, we were still on rations whilst the French had everything'. This picture of opportunities for some youngsters outside the formal curriculum is supported by HMI. They wrote of a secondary school in Newcastle running exchange trips to Denmark, and a Bristol grammar school arranging visits to Switzerland, Germany, Belgium, the Yorkshire Dales, Skye, Wales, and the Lakes as well as numerous trips to local theatres.

Susan Rear described how a Shakespeare play and a Gilbert and Sullivan opera were produced in alternate years in her grammar school on the outskirts of Leeds. One year the school put on a play by Sophocles, possibly to help two Oxbridge hopefuls gain familiarity with the classics!

Many others remembered individual teachers who supported them, if not always with affection, certainly with respect. Dr. Hazel Russman recalled many teachers in her North London grammar as 'single women from the generation that had lost their sweethearts in the first world war. We may not have liked them but we respected them'. Dr. Ian Keil was enthused by a new young English teacher at his school who 'encouraged me to have my own opinions'. He gave Ian the editorship of the school magazine, and this he said, 'added greatly to my self-confidence'.

If these comments suggest an age of optimism in education, others are less so. Of the 280 or so responses, about 40 per cent offered a largely negative image of the writers' time at school. I had expected fewer unfavourable views, for several reasons. First, the group was obviously self-selected which meant that, whilst many had strong views on their education, none was wholly indifferent to the subject or apathetic about the value of school in general. The absence of this view would reduce the number of negative responses. Secondly, the group was not representative of the school population of the period because women, ex-grammar school pupils and bright secondary modern pupils were over-represented and men and academically weaker pupils under-represented in the sample. Overall, women and ex-grammar school pupils who responded were more positive about their schooling than men and secondary modern pupils. Also there is the tendency for older people to look back at their youth through rose-tinted spectacles.

The main areas of criticism raised were low expectations, often linked to social class, unduly harsh and/or unfair treatment by teachers, lack of pastoral care and poor guidance and careers advice.

Low expectations of children from poorer backgrounds were almost as prevalent in grammar schools as in the secondary moderns. Adele Winston writes of her London grammar school,

> We had a council flat in Hackney, (my parents) were undaunted by the fact that until comparatively recently the school had been fee-paying...we could scarcely afford the fares let alone the uniform. It was made abundantly clear by the wretched women who taught us that they were doing us a huge favour by teaching us at all. I left after the fourth form and until quite recently imagined that the other girls had gone to university. In fact having read law at Cardiff and graduated in 1996 I seem to have been the only one of my contemporaries to have gone on to higher things.

Pat Taylor, another working-class girl, attended a prestigious grammar school in the north-east but was refused entry to the sixth form despite having passed 9 O-levels, a tremendous achievement for the day. The headmistress claimed this was because her results were not good enough, despite then admitting twins from a local independent school with only six O-levels between them! Pat knew the real reason was that, '..after O-level it was expected that all the working-class girls would leave quickly and get respectable office jobs'. Only after her mother sought an interview with the director of education was the decision reversed and Pat allowed into the sixth form where she flourished as 'the only working-class fly in the high fliers ointment'.

Even those who made it to the sixth form could not always escape such attitudes. A woman who attended a Lincolnshire grammar school was one of only two girls from her large pre-fab council estate to do so and spoke with 'a thick Lincolnshire accent'. She was shocked and 'livid' to accidentally see a school document describing her as 'not university material', despite her having 8 O-level passes and 3 anticipated good A-level passes which she achieved. Jennifer Elliott de Riverol, who went to a secondary modern and then on to a grammar school sixth form, says 'I was certainly aware of the class system where pupils from the working classes were not expected to do well academically'. Strangely, this particular form of social engineering or political correctness seems to have escaped newspapers then which are so exercised by the issue today. Nor do these accounts sit easily with the claim that working-class children, whilst under-represented in grammar schools, were at least guaranteed a straightforward route up the social ladder once they had overcome the 11+ hurdle. How many working-class mothers would have had the tenacity or confidence to pursue the issue of Pat Taylor's admission to the sixth form as her's did?

Predictably, the lowest expectations of pupils' prospects were found in the secondary modern schools. It was a tough task for teachers as huge numbers of children were left with a sense of hopelessness after the 11+ results emerged. Brenda Morrison, later reassessed for a technical school, was first sent to a London school 'regarded as a sink school for failures like me'. Although many teachers and heads worked tirelessly to restore self-esteem and maintain the work ethic, not all succeeded and sadly some did not even try. Geoffrey Bennett, at school on the south coast, was never given a single piece of homework in his entire school life and often 'wasted time as there was little or no supervision'. Olive Taylor in London recalls 'whole classes spent in idle chatter as the teachers talked in groups in the corridor'. My father-in-law recounted how a local authority inspector arrived unannounced during lesson time at a boys' secondary modern school in Bradford to find almost the entire staff playing cards, whilst pupils wandered the building unsupervised.

Paul Brinklow recalls his secondary schooling in north London as a time of 'all discipline and little learning'. Mrs S.Ashton, from the north west, recounts the amazement of her own children, both graduates, at her lack of opportunities at school. An ex-pupil of a west midlands girls' secondary modern, who was in the A stream, writes: 'more was expected but not that much... I was left with the feeling that we were given just enough education to fulfil our basic needs eg to get a job in a factory until we got married'.

Many at school at this time angrily recalled the casual violence which characterised their childhood. Don McCullin, the war photographer, says flatly that his teachers were bullies. 'We knew only violence, ignorance and brutality.' (*TES*, 03/12/04)

Few correspondents objected on principle to corporal punishment, most supporting it for serious offences but there were numerous references to unofficial actions, unacceptable even by the standards of the day let alone the present. These were not simply flying chalk and board dusters, which most children shrugged off.

Cases like an ex-marine giving a boy a bloody nose with a back hander or the teacher who delighted in giving vicious karate chops to pupils' necks, leading one father to complain formally, make uncomfortable reading. Often such behaviour seemed to arise simply from personal dislike of a particular child, as with the London boy who moved to school in Wales and was regularly tripped up by a certain teacher as he left class. Edward Blishen, teaching in a boys' urban secondary modern, recounted how when 'passing between rows of boys on normal occasions, I found this one or that instinctively ducking. The mere proximity of an adult had this effect on some boys' (Blishen, 1955 p29).

On the website for ex-pupils of my own school, one contributor tells how he was felled to the ground by a massive punch by one of the Christian Brothers who ran the school. Some contributors to the website viewed its eventual closure and demolition in the 80s as a young Jane Eyre or Smike might have regarded the demise of Lowood school or Dotheboys Hall. One wrote

> After having had **40 years** to reflect, I still regard the five years at De La Salle as the worst of my life. I remember my only return to the site when I went, with deep satisfaction, to view a pile of rubble.

Even where corporal punishment was inflicted in a manner deemed appropriate for the day, it was often neither fair nor a last resort. Stephanie Lowe describes being caned for getting a sum wrong but moments later the teacher realised her answer had been correct after all. She was called out to the front and the cross in her book next to the sum was altered to a tick, without a word. Stephanie began to cry, not because of the punishment but because of the teacher's failure to apologise or offer a single consoling word. She was then caned again for over-reacting. The use of cane or strap as a casual teaching aid in maths lessons was common. Ted Martin told of some teachers who 'seemed to delight in caning', including one who caned any pupil 'who could not solve the problem on the board when hauled to the front.' Ted added ' this happened to me frequently and did nothing to improve my maths.'

Jon Pound, at school in Lancashire, recalled another maths teacher who 'gave you a stroke of the cane for every question you got wrong'. Jon remembered getting the cane up to six times in half and hour and ended, with dry understatement, 'I don't think he was qualified to teach the subject'.

In my third year I had a maths teacher who routinely used the strap to punish the most trivial of offences, such as making a blot or drawing a crooked line. One boy had an essential tremor in the hand and would hold up his book, covered in smudges, for those behind to see before the inevitable punishment. It was difficult to see how hitting him repeatedly on that same hand would help his affliction. Some thirty years later I was appointed head of a new Catholic comprehensive school. Prior to its opening an elderly parish priest from a town some distance away saw me and stressed the importance of pastoral care in the new school. He said 'The parents will want you to look after their children and cherish them as much as they would.'

As he was leaving he remarked, 'You haven't recognised me but we have met before. I used to be a maths teacher: I taught you in the third year...' I was silent for a few moments, recalling the boy with the tremor. Then, as I bade him farewell I assured him that we would indeed cherish the children in the new school.

Lack of pastoral care or interest in the lives of pupils outside the classroom concerned a number of correspondents who felt, like Susan Lindley at a bi-lateral school in South Yorkshire, that almost 'all of her teachers were un-approachable'. Adele Winston said that because she was poor at games, she was bullied beyond belief, with the teacher's involvement and approval, whilst Olive Taylor was scathing about the 'disregard by the staff for the welfare of their charges'. A correspondent from Hertfordshire described how her adoptive mother had died when she was thirteen and, apart from a letter of condolence to her adoptive father, 'the matter was never mentioned again. No pastoral care at all'. Isabella Palmer was bullied at her Sunderland secondary modern and asked if she could leave five minutes early to avoid the bullies: this was refused and she became 'ever more withdrawn'. She writes 'I often think if our teachers had been more friendly, as they are today I would have done a lot better'.

An almost universal criticism of schools at this time, even from those who have only praise for other aspects of their schooling, involves the poor advice on careers and children's future beyond school. One writer from London, who regarded his London grammar school as a 'very good school', speaks of the 'wholly inadequate preparation of boys for the world of (non-university) work'. Ron Wilson, who has largely happy memories of his secondary modern in the north-east believes that his education, 'came up woefully short at the end' in terms of careers advice. Whilst not blaming his school, he felt strongly that 'the fact there were thousands of occupations that boys like myself could have tried and been successful at seemed of little consequence'. Another writer spoke of the 'narrow corridors of choice'. Women who were at grammar schools at the time condemned with one voice the lack of career choices offered other than teaching or nursing.

Poor careers advice was linked with a wider lack of accountability to parents and a failure to value their role in education. Parents' evenings did not exist in some schools. Reports to parents were often extraordinarily perfunctory and often opaque. Even the famed wit and biting sarcasm which is often quoted in the school reports of the great and the good were not as prevalent as imagined. My own reports cover three years at grammar school, years 2, 3 and 4. The total number of words in five reports is 163: this includes counting the ubiquitous 'v', as in 'very', as a full word! In the summer of 1957, my report for ten subjects consisted of only 30 words. In contrast many modern reports contain several hundred words. Nine of the 30 words in 1957 were from the chemistry teacher, who wrote, 'Improving. Some practice in drawing would not be wasted', probably the only constructive, if startingly irrelevant, criticism I received in a report. This was typical. One secondary school report I received did reach a heady 88 words but others totalled around 35.

In the 50s not all schools produced reports and certainly HMI did not comment on the quality of reporting to parents or indeed on relations between schools and parents. However, although pastoral care, expectations of pupils and links with parents are vital, it is the quality of teaching and learning which lies at the heart of the success or failure of any school system.

4
Teaching and learning in the 1950s and 1960s

British governments have claimed that Ofsted has provided a fuller picture of the state of teaching and learning than exists anywhere in the world. Not everyone agrees. Some argue that the view from Ofsted is too rosy and that many inspectors have 'gone native'. Other critics, like the late Ted Wragg, believed that the organisation is too bureaucratic, obsessed with statistics, and recognises the measurable rather than the important. Whatever the truth, a great deal of time and money has been spent in evaluating schools in the last decade or so, especially the quality of teaching and learning. If there is a lack of consensus about what is happening today, how much more difficult is it to judge the standards of classroom practice of fifty years ago?

In an attempt to do this I examined several types of evidence: the correspondence from *Saga* readers, major reports such as those of Crowther and Newsom, plus unpublished Ministry of Education material in the National Archives (NA). The main sources of evidence were HMI reports of inspections of schools. I looked at 305 reports from 24 local authorities (NA ED/109/various) mostly covering the years 1955 to 1961, although a few dated back to 1952. I sought to ensure a representative coverage of different types of local authorities: county and borough, rural, urban as well as a good geographical and socio-economic coverage.

The local education authorities whose school reports I examined were:

County Boroughs	Counties
Bradford	Cheshire
Birmingham	Cumberland
Bristol	Derbyshire

Hull	Devon
Leeds	Dorset
Newcastle	Essex
Liverpool	Hampshire
Middlesbrough	Lincolnshire (Holland)
Oldham	Middlesex
Sheffield	North Riding (Yorkshire)
Swansea	Surrey
	West Sussex
London	

The reports differed significantly from those of Ofsted today. They were confidential to the school and local authority. It is more difficult to compare HMI's views of different schools because the style was more individual than that of modern reports. Although common evaluative terms such as 'good', 'satisfactory' or 'poor' appear, they are not consistently used. HMI were given free rein to express themselves and often did so in idiosyncratic terms. At one secondary modern school in Middlesex, the reporting inspector, as the senior HMI on an inspection was known, listed every department under evaluative headings of his own: 'a little above average', 'satisfactory', 'humdrum', 'weak' and 'poor'. As no department was graded better than 'a little above average', it must have been a pretty humdrum school.

The conclusion of reports sometimes conflict with the findings on individual departments often sounding less critical. In a Bristol grammar school inspected in November 1958, HMI concluded that a 'tradition of sound work had been built up' notwithstanding critical reports on English, French, geography and art, and highly critical reports on science, maths, German and music. The 'sound work' seems to have been restricted to history and PE! HMI in the 50s were also prepared to give schools in difficult circumstances the benefit of the doubt in terms which would be politically unacceptable today. Many teachers now argue that the social and economic challenges facing some schools are insufficiently recognised by Ofsted. But phrases such as the following, which would never appear today, were commonplace in the 50s.

> 'The problems of this school are the problems of a large municipal housing estate.' (Girls' secondary modern, Birmingham, March 1956)

> 'In a school such as this, it is impossible to judge progress by academic achievement.' (Girls' secondary modern, Leeds, January 1956)

> 'The difficulties of this school arise from the problems of the area.' (Boys' secondary modern, London, January 1956)

In keeping with this generous approach there are frequent references to the promise of improvement in the future. A Hampshire secondary modern 'contains many promising features for future development'. A headteacher in a Devon secondary modern in October 1959, '...clearly has the welfare of the school at heart and is anxious to raise its prestige'. This would surely apply to most head teachers and tells us little about his effectiveness. Indeed, HMI saw a major part of their role as encouragement. Reports often have the military flavour of morale boosting chats to the troops from senior officers. Orchestras are 'gallant', masters in inner city schools do 'loyal work', teaching is 'sincere' and suburban girls' schools are 'busy, cheerful places'. Despite these caveats there is ample evidence to allow conclusions to be drawn about the overall quality of teaching and learning and these are summarised as follows

- Teaching in most schools was satisfactory or even better. But the proportion of poor teaching was significantly larger than today and the worst was truly dreadful

- The curriculum was far narrower than today, with many subjects and areas of study now regarded as essential being dropped at an early age

- Opportunities for girls were astonishingly limited, to a greater extent than appreciated today

- There was strong emphasis on the teaching of the basics: grammar, spelling and punctuation in English plus the rudiments of arithmetic. But the outcomes were frequently unsuccessful. Illiteracy, though sharply reduced since the war, was still widespread in the 50s and certainly not eradicated, as some now claim

- The teaching of mathematics was rarely better than mediocre: for many pupils including most girls, it was dire

- Even in the better schools, both secondary modern and grammar, there was a great deal of uninspired, unchallenging teaching including copying from blackboards or textbooks

- The quality of leadership provided by headteachers and governors to classroom teachers was variable. Whilst there were many outstanding heads, men and women of intellect, vision and determination, others were limited in outlook, grossly incompetent and some were bullies. As with the weakest classroom teachers, the worst were so bad that today they would be quickly removed

Whilst it is impossible to assess the quality of schools from past HMI reports on the four point scale which is used by Ofsted today, it is obvious which schools inspectors regarded as good or unsatisfactory overall. Most schools in the 50s were successful and HMI were delighted to say so, as these examples indicate:

'This is a hard-working, happy and successful school with good social standards and an intellectual vitality.' (North Riding grammar school, March 1954)

'A strongly directed and vigorous school exercising a valuable influence in a predominantly artisan neighbourhood.' (Birmingham secondary modern, November 1956)

'This vital school thoroughly deserves the high regard in which it is held.' (Hull secondary modern, February 1959)

and

'The school maintains its deservedly high reputation for academic achievement.' (Newcastle direct grant grammar, October 1956)

HMI were clear about why schools were successful. Two Newcastle secondary moderns succeeded as a result, in one case (May 1957), of the 'primary belief that no pupil should be allowed to feel herself a failure' and in the second, inspected a few months later, 'the quality of the work... arises from the conviction of the staff that what they teach is valuable... Most staff are skilful classroom teachers'. The best teachers left an impression which has lasted half a century. A correspondent, Eileen Elstrop recalled Mr.Whalley, her English teacher at a Whitby secondary modern, contributing 'so much to her love of books', including the Brontes. Ted Martin remembered an inspirational history teacher who inspired a life long enthusiasm for American history. HMI referred often to teachers triumphing over adversity, many working heroically in appalling conditions. Ed Adams, another correspondent, teaching in an under-resourced, gloomy, secondary modern in a poor district of Leeds, set up a school radio station which was financed by the sale of empty jam jars and broadcast interviews with local personalities, including the chief constable.

Yet despite the inspectors' forgiving approach and understandable reluctance to condemn schools which were working with the most disadvantaged, what they witnessed was often so alarming that they did not pull their punches. It was not hard to determine which schools were, in modern parlance, failing to provide a satisfactory education.

I adopted two indicators of inadequacy. First, that the general conclusion of the report indicated serious weaknesses affecting the performance of the whole school or, secondly, that there were at least four unsatisfactory departments, including maths or English. In practice, both indicators applied to almost all the schools which I classed as failing.

The following examples are typical of many comments on inadequate schools.

'There are real weaknesses. Efforts are uncoordinated. Much clearer guidance is needed from the headteacher and heads of subjects on the content of courses and teaching methods.' (Bradford boys' secondary modern, July 1959)

In addition, there were serious criticisms of English, maths, science, social studies, art and woodwork.

'The standard of work is nowhere high. There is a tendency to underestimate the girls both in their academic work and in their roles as responsible people.' (Hull girls' secondary modern, April 1960)

'Years of further difficulty lie ahead. [The school needs to] enliven interest and make more rigorous demands on the boys.' (Cheshire boys' grammar school, March 1955)

'Concerted efforts are needed to raise academic standards.' (There were also strong criticisms of English, maths, geography, French, art and PE) (Girls' secondary modern, Hampshire, November 1959)

'Many pupils waste time in school..(the school's) present condition does not reflect its true potential.' (London secondary modern, October 1958)

'Problems with academic studies, as well as education in the widest sense, remain.' (Liverpool RC boys' grammar, May 1956)

'The last report drew attention to weaknesses in staffing, organisation, standards and discipline. It cannot be said the school has advanced.' (Liverpool mixed RC secondary modern, December 1959)

In addition, there were critical reports on English, maths, science, history, geography and art. No metal or woodwork was being taught and the music teacher was 'away' during the inspection.

'The quality of the work is as indifferent as their (the pupils') attitude is casual'. (West Sussex boys' secondary modern, February 1959)

'There are many able and hard-working children in the school. At present they are not being given the opportunity to develop their skills or intellectual abilities. There is a need for the headmaster to give a strong lead to the staff on teaching methods and standards of work.' (Essex secondary modern, May 1957)

In addition to the main reports HMI also made a verbatim record of the formal discussion on their findings with governors and the headteacher at the end of the inspection. Sometimes these minutes give a better insight into the inspectors' true opinion of a school than the actual report. A Middlesex boys school was described as 'doing steady work within its powers' but in discussion afterwards the reporting inspector said that teaching in five of the seventeen forms was 'very weak', a proportion which would lead to a school being placed in special measures today.

Elsewhere differences between the report and the oral comments were subtler but still significant. In a report on a Leeds girls' grammar school, HMI concluded that 'It remains for the headmistress to create the conditions in which attitudes towards learning can be fully developed' whereas in discussion with the governors, comments were sharper: 'The picture of achievement is below what the girls should be producing over five years'.

The overall picture of the quality of teaching and learning from this sample of 305 reports is extremely mixed. Apart from schools clearly thought to be unsatisfactory by HMI, there were many others where the work is described only as 'sound', 'satisfactory' or 'average'. Sometimes assessments sound dismissive and patronising to the modern reader. In a Bermondsey secondary modern the head teacher had 'realised the humble mentality of his pupils and set... the work accordingly', whilst in a Middlesex school, HMI told governors that the work in the school was 'dull and plodding ...in accordance with the abilities of the staff'.

Where there was ambiguity about whether HMI regarded a school as failing I gave it the benefit of the doubt. Nevertheless the overall figures make stark reading. Of the 305 schools whose reports I reviewed, 61 (20%) were clearly regarded as inadequate by the inspectors – a much higher figure than today. The percentage of unsatisfactory grammar and technical grammar schools in the sample was similar to that of failing secondary moderns. Although no comprehensive and bi-lateral schools in the sample were failing, the numbers were too small to be significant. The number of grammar schools which were criticised might surprise some but whilst this could have been the result of a less tolerant attitude by HMI towards weaknesses in selective schools, individual subject reports on many grammar schools often paint a bleak picture.

Table 2: Sample of HMI reports 1952-61

	Total	Failing/unsatisfactory	
All schools inspected in sample	305	61	(20%)
Grammar and technical grammar schools	75	15	(20%)
Secondary modern schools	224	46	(21%)
Others	6	0	

A similar picture emerged in the accounts of many correspondents who made contact through *Saga magazine*. As with HMI most comments were positive, although a few regarded a good teacher as anyone who could maintain total silence in class for forty minutes, almost regardless of the value of the lesson!

But a sizeable group had very negative views of the teaching they received. Anthony Dunn recalls his time at a grammar school in Gloucestershire

> The teaching was really rather poor... Little marking was done and often the lessons were simply regurgitation of the teacher's notes from when they themselves were at school. One or two just had their old exercise books propped up on their briefcases. A number had little control, one or two were pathetically weak, being played up the whole school day. I don't think preparation of lessons came into their thinking.

Sheila Lunn, in a grammar stream at a secondary modern in Wimbledon, remembers her teachers 'as not very inspiring' and an excellent biology teacher as the one 'bright star in our week' compared with the dreaded dull monotone of the woman who taught chemistry and physics. Carole Alston, at an Essex secondary modern, felt the quality of teaching was poor:

> I cannot recall having a conversation with any subject teacher and only spoke when asked a question. It was very easy to get left behind..because teaching just rolled on and nobody catered for the young person who failed to grasp it.

Dennis Cooke attended an 'average' grammar school in the 50s where the 'teaching was at best mediocre and frequently poor' (*The Guardian*, 21/11/05).

Although I received some excellent teaching, especially in the sixth form, the worst was appalling and would be unacceptable today. At the start of my second year our English teacher told us we were to write a novel. We had no instruction on what was expected and didn't have a clue how to approach the task. We were given empty exercise books and told to get on with it. Week after week, month after month, dozens of lessons were taken up with thirty or so boys writing in silence, on and on, whilst the teacher sat and read to himself at the front. The exercise books were only taken in at the end of the year. Needless to say we never saw our work again. One can imagine the horror of an Ofsted inspector faced with such a charade today and wonder what would appear in his or her report!

Only when I researched this topic fifty years later did I uncover an explanation for the teacher's behaviour. In an HMI report on the school a few months earlier the English inspector had complained that, '..the different aspects of English were treated in isolation.. in some lower forms no essays were written in the first half of the year'. Perhaps the English teacher told the staff common room 'Well if that's what they want, I'll make the little blighters write a whole novel!'

The curriculum offered in many schools was narrow and constrained with pressure being put on pupils to drop subjects early on. 'There were weak-nesses', recalled Anthony Dunn, 'because of the choice system...I have no science because I did Latin and Greek'. John Riley, who was at school in Woolstanton, was also critical of the arts/science divide. Even in grammar schools the curriculum created a sharp divide between 'sheep and goats'. Adele Winston reflected on how streaming at her London school dictated not only the pace of learning but timetabling and the curriculum.

> Latin for the clever girls, German for the middle layer and domestic science for the rest despite the fact they had all passed the 11plus and (the school) was over-subscribed.

Surprisingly, several people recalled the low status of music. At Pat Clayton's grammar school it was

> not taught at all... The weekly lesson consisted of the class getting round a piano and singing whatever the cathedral organist decided we would sing at the end of term.

Ian Keil wrote that there was 'little effort to engage pupils in any systematic learning about any aspect of music' at his Wiltshire school. And HMI res-ponded sharply to the governor of a Bristol grammar school who claimed that 'girls needed music more than boys'. 'Here' he responded 'the boys don't even know how to sing a hymn'.

The deficiencies of 1950s education were most apparent in the education of girls. But for a few it was a time of increased opportunity, exemplified by Christine Jackson's teachers at her Oxfordshire grammar school, who were 'dedicated and interested in our progress' and who warned their girls that 'they would meet opposition but attitudes would eventually change'. However, the practice of teaching girls domestic science whilst the boys did wood-work and metalwork was accepted by even the most enlightened teachers at the time.

What did concern HMI and others was the widespread practice of girls fol-lowing reduced science courses or not being taught science at all. Challenged by HMI on why girls were not doing science, the head of a mixed secondary modern in Tottenham, responded with sublime indifference, '...my science staff can't handle girls'.

Other references to the treatment of girls as second class citizens would sur-prise even the most chauvinist today. One mixed Devon secondary modern school, inspected in June 1958, had only just ended the practice (in time for the inspection?) of allowing only boys to go on trips and visits outside the school gates! The boys were also always served dinner first. One lady governor in a Derbyshire secondary school was 'speechless with rage' to learn that the girls' playground had been entirely taken over for a new science laboratory and no alternative provision made. It seemed that the boys' play area would not have been annexed.

Even the attitude of some heads to girls' education created anxiety. The governor of a mixed Birmingham grammar school where inspectors had commented on the 'marked disparity' between the standards of boys and of girls stated flatly, 'The head is not interested in the achievement of the girls'. HMI did not contradict him. It was girls who were allowed or compelled to drop maths astonishingly early, a practice which today would be as un-thinkable as it would be illegal. Penny Grimes, at a Kent secondary modern, had dropped maths by the age of 14. Margaret Abraham's tutor in an FE college she attended from the age of 15 'had great difficulty believing that she had simply been excluded from this subject'. Janet Lateu also gave up maths when she transferred to a north east grammar school.

HMI reports make numerous references to girls not studying maths throughout their time at school, in grammar schools as well as secondary moderns. HMI reported that in a Newcastle girls' grammar in May 1956 only 'a few girls who find maths difficult discontinue the subject at the end of the fourth year'. Yet at a similar school elsewhere in the city, they noted that 'in the fourth and fifth year many drop the subject entirely' (November 1958). In a school which only catered for the top 20 per cent or so of the ability range it had been decided that 'many' pupils would drop maths after only three years. This sits uneasily with the claim that, unlike today, this was a time when the true importance of the basics was recognised.

In reality, for all the apparent emphasis on the basics of literacy – grammar, punctuation, spelling and handwriting – HMI were often unimpressed by outcomes on the ground. In one North Riding grammar school '...the frequency of spelling errors in the sixth form is too great and sentence structure often insecure' (March 1954). In a second, 'none of the work (in English) is distinguished and the pupils are not accurate on paper' (June 1952). At a girls' secondary modern in Leeds pupils '.. find it difficult to write fluently; their efforts are sparse and lack originality', in another secondary modern in Devon 'errors mar so much written work' (June 1958) and a third, in Enfield, had 'low standards of presentation, handwriting, spelling and punctuation' (October 1956). In a technical grammar school in Essex, HMI noted that 'too much time is spent on formal grammatical work they (pupils) find hard if not impossible' (May 1956).

In many schools time was spent on achingly dull, repetitive exercises, as at the Liverpool secondary modern where English was 'unduly formalised in a way that does not lead to a transference of grammatical knowledge in practice' (December 1959).

Frequently the end result was neither a sound grasp of basic literacy nor an appreciation of the joy of English literature nor any opportunity to write independently. A Sheffield grammar school was typical of many where HMI noted that 'a strong emphasis on language exercises has not even produced a high level of mechanical accuracy' (February 1956). 'The beauty of the spoken word does not have the place it deserves', reported the inspectors at a Hampshire grammar school in May 1957.

Ten months earlier they had seen little 'of the teaching of literature in the lower forms' at a grammar school in Middlesex and thought that a couple of prose books a year was 'a frugal diet' at a Newcastle technical school in June 1956. In a Middlesex secondary modern the 'opportunities of enjoyment of literature, poetry and drama' were too limited' (March 1956). The Newsom report, commenting on English teaching in the early 60s, noted that 'free composition produces a shapeless mess..the memory of many televised westerns... still riding on the range of pupils' minds' (Newsom, 1963 p152).

Even where teaching was competent, as it was in a Bradford secondary modern inspected in July 1959, it often 'lacked variety and failed to stimulate response from the pupils'. Inspectors repeatedly commented how much of the work, whilst dull, also lacked challenge. In a boys' secondary modern school in Middlesex, English 'demanded too little effort from the boys and failed to arouse their interest' (January 1956) whilst in a similar school in West

Sussex, 'the tempo of the work is too slow and does not present sufficient challenge'. (February 1959).

Elsewhere more fortunate youngsters enjoyed a better experience, like those at an Essex secondary modern school where English was 'carefully taught' by staff who took a 'delight in poetry and are able to communicate their appreciation of it'. A *Saga* correspondent, Jackie Goode, offered a moving account of her English teacher

> He used his own wit to motivate and delight us by sharing his enthusiasm for his subject whether we were involved in parsing or Prester John. What perhaps epitomises his ability to communicate his love (for literature and poetry) are those times we were allowed to close our eyes and simply listen to his reading of chosen texts, ranging from James Thurber's *Walter Mitty* to Paul Gallico's *The Snow Goose*. Wonderful, wonderful simply to listen and drink in the words and their meanings.

But overall HMI had serious concerns about the quality of the teaching of English in almost a third of schools inspected, a very high figure by today's standards.

A major preoccupation today is the extent of illiteracy. Many commentators claim that the situation is worse than it was half a century ago. Some government documents of the time imply that by the 1950s illiteracy was no longer seen as a major problem. Surveys for the Ministry of Defence suggested that illiteracy amongst National Service recruits was under 1 per cent, whilst the Ministry of Education Annual Report for 1957 stated that illiteracy was nearly non-existent in England and Wales (Ministry of Education, 1957-8 p559).

But definitions of literacy vary greatly over time. The benchmark for literacy was set much lower than the present day 'expected' level 4 of the National Curriculum for 11 year-olds. The National Service test merely asked recruits to read an instruction to write down their basic personal details and then to do so (Ministry of Education, 1957 Appendix IV p44). The 1957 report, whilst claiming that illiteracy had indeed been almost eradicated, added a telling rider. It compared illiteracy in English to that in a foreign language. There were, indeed, hardly any illiterate children in '... the sense that the average Englishman cannot read a word of Arabic'

If either of these elementary definitions were used by ministers or educationalists today as evidence of rising standards the derision of opposition parties and the media would ring across the land. Furthermore the requirement for literacy amongst the work force, whilst rising after the war, was still far less than today. Today much of the perceived problem is due to the improvement in literacy rates not keeping pace with the rise in the requirement for literacy. This is true both in breadth and depth: in terms of the proportion of the workforce needing to be literate, which is virtually 100 per cent, and the degree of literacy now required of those who could formerly have carried out their duties with basic literacy skills.

An internal Ministry document from the time says that 'a 1955 London County Council survey gave no ground at all for much happiness about the standards of literacy amongst many modern school leavers,' whilst also noting the large number of school leavers with a reading age of 9 or less (NA. Ed, 147/565). It is also probable that much illiteracy after the war was hidden The lack of any national collation of absence figures make it likely many struggling pupils, miserable at their lack of progress, simply truanted and were not included in any surveys. Nowadays all published national statistics of tests and examinations, significantly, count absentees as failures.

Even so there is evidence of widespread illiteracy in HMI reports of the time, as revealed in the following

> 'Reading ability is poor.... by the end of their school careers few pupils can be considered established as readers or writers.' (Birmingham secondary modern, November 1956)

> 'There is a problem of illiteracy.' (Birmingham secondary modern, March 1958)

> '...problems of illiteracy persist into the fourth year.' (Cheshire secondary modern school, July 1956)

> 'The school is successful in enabling girls who could barely read on entry to make some progress.' (London girls' secondary modern, October 1957)

> 'A few boys in each form cannot read... but there is no serious non-reading issue.' (Liverpool RC boys' secondary modern, February 1956)

> 'Reading presents few difficulties except in 1C.' (Leeds secondary modern, February 1956). But note that 1C represented one third of the initial intake.

> 'Many boys write with difficulty.' (Cheshire grammar school, March 1958)

The problem was not only an urban one. In a Devon secondary modern, HMI reported in May 1956 that 'Form 1 pupils are learning to read', and elsewhere in the county '...some boys are seriously retarded in reading' (March 1960). At a third school a governor claimed, during the post-inspection meeting, that in several neighbouring schools most children left unable to read or write.

Neither HMI nor the Chief Education Officer contradicted him and at another meeting the following year, at a school described as 'barely satisfactory', the CEO stated that the county desperately needed special educational needs teachers in its secondary schools but could not afford them.

Notes from senior civil servants also show little confidence that illiteracy had disappeared.

> What the general public suspects is that, even disregarding the girls and boys of poor home background etc., there remain people capable of learning [to read] who do not make proper progress. The public... suspect that this may be due to rank bad teaching, lack of discipline, too many activities and so on. (NA ED, 147/566)

If the teaching of English gave rise to concerns in many schools, mathematics was in an even worse condition almost everywhere. Whilst critical reports on English represented a substantial minority, around a third, it is rare to find any strong praise of maths, regardless of type of school or location. Of the HMI reports reviewed around half tell of maths departments which were failing, had serious weaknesses or were just satisfactory. Similarly, only a small minority of correspondents contacted via *Saga magazine* enjoyed maths lessons and many wrote about leaving school with no real grasp of the subject.

The same weaknesses are identified by HMI across the country. The teaching was repetitious, pupils constantly revising work already covered in primary school. As a result, abler pupils were never stretched and the problems of weaker pupils not addressed as they failed repeatedly at the same tasks, despite the severe approach of some teachers. Strong criticisms of the maths lessons in some schools were made by HMI in every single one of the education authorities whose inspection reports were examined. These extracts are typical of dozens

> 'The teaching lacks inspiration, direction and unity of purpose. More thought should be given to the needs of the less able.' (Hampshire secondary modern, February 1956)

> 'Although all boys follow the O-level course quite a number experience such difficulty that they do not sit the examination... a number find difficulties which prove insuperable. Less time [should] be devoted to the revision of primary school work.' (Cheshire grammar school, March 1958)

> '...pupils show an insecure grasp of the fundamentals.' (Derbyshire secondary modern, July 1960)

'Even abler pupils suffer from a lack of confidence in mental processes.' (London secondary modern, June 1958)

'Maths is not a strength of this school.' (North Riding grammar school, 1956)

'The course did not have much meaning for the less able pupils and ...failed to make adequate demands on the abler ones.' (Bristol secondary modern, March 1956)

'The work is mainly elementary arithmetic from books more suitable for primary children.' (Swansea secondary modern, March 1956)

'..failure of teachers to diagnose the disabilities of many pupils.' (Newcastle secondary modern, May 1957)

'Little development from primary school...a weak subject.' (Cheshire secondary modern, May 1957)

'Some masters have a great deal to learn in the matter of techniques...too little demand on the boys.' (London boys' secondary modern, March 1957)

'Considerable (time) is spent on the revision of fractions and decimals but few pupils attain any facility in applying them.' (Middlesex secondary modern, April 1956)

'Many.. leave school ill-equipped to deal with everyday matters of money and measurement.' (Middlesex secondary modern, October 1956)

'Insufficient attention paid to mathematical accuracy.. too much repetition of elementary processes... thought needs to be given to diagnosis of individual weaknesses.' (Surrey secondary modern, March 1959)

It is hardly surprising that the government's Skills for Life Survey in 2005 found half of all 55 to 65 year-olds had only the maths skills expected nowadays of a 9 year-old. The weaknesses in maths in girls' schools are underlined by the finding that women from this age group were much more likely than men to have problems with basic maths.

Other curriculum subjects also faced serious problems. Science teachers struggled against numerous constraints: the lack of well-equipped laboratories, shortages of qualified staff and, even in an age of huge scientific advances internationally, an ambivalence amongst many heads and governors about the subject's worth in the curriculum.

HMI were appreciative where schools were making genuine efforts against all the odds. In a Bermondsey secondary modern, 'two young teachers without qualifications are courageously attempting to cover the subject' (May 1957). Elsewhere they criticised the absence of practical work, reliance on copied notes and serious health and safety issues, including unearthed electrical equipment and easily accessible poisons.

In a Devon secondary modern where the pupils had little interest in science and the 'untidy copying of notes' played a much larger part than experimentation, the inspector called for a 'new and livelier approach'. One girl, whose voice decades later can still be heard rising in irritation, would have enthusiastically endorsed this

> I don't like science. About plants and how they breathe. I'm not interested in that! I'm not interested in how plants breathe. I don't care how they do it ...I've had enough school! (Dobinson, 1963 p13)

HMI inspected science teaching throughout Swansea and found it unsatisfactory in all the town's secondary modern schools. The main reasons were a lack of teaching competence and differentiation, an over-academic approach and too much reliance on copied notes.

According to both inspectors and those at school in the 50s, dull copying of material from the blackboard or, even more pointlessly, from textbooks already in the pupils' possession, occupied hours of school time, especially in humanities subjects, such as history, geography and religious studies. History, according to Ofsted, is now one of the best taught subjects in school. This was not always so. An assessment of history teaching between the wars has shown that nearly 30 per cent of lessons were unsatisfactory, a huge figure by today's standards for any subject. (Elliott, 1975). HMI found that a quarter of London secondary pupils in 1926 were unable to write a short account of even two historical persons or events, chosen by themselves. A survey of history in Leicestershire schools revealed that the pupils' 'mental picture was hazy.... history was a jumble of disconnected facts'. 'Napoleon fought at the battle of Bosworth in 1660,' hazarded one pupil, recalling at least some local history!

Little appeared to have changed in many schools by the 50s and 60s: HMI described history in a Lincolnshire grammar school in May 1961

> Undue emphasis on the oral exposition of the textbook, memorisation of dictated notes.. interest rarely stimulated... examination results are disappointing.... sixth form work mediocre.

There are constant references to history being dull and 'arid'. Even the deadly copied notes were 'lacking clarity and precision' (Cheshire grammar school 1958). Some who remember their school days fondly, like Suzanne Hanks, still found history, geography and religious studies boring whilst Geoffrey Bennett 'longed to learn some history'. Stephanie Lowe recalls how her history teacher 'leaned against the radiator and talked for 45 minutes. Nothing was ever written on the board. We all fell asleep and dropped history after two years'. Penny Grimes said her history teacher in Ashford 'spent my GCE year chatting about her forthcoming wedding' – possibly a welcome change from copying notes.

Practical and creative subjects like art, woodwork and metalwork suffered from the same lack of facilities in many schools as science, with staff often forced to teach in conditions which few today would accept. Inspectors spoke of the severe strain on one Bristol art teacher of working in a 'cold, damp room' and elsewhere the head's study doubled as the art storeroom. Art, regarded by Ofsted now as the best taught subject, was often a poor relation. Pat Clayton remembers her art teaching as 'hopeless' and adds 'if anyone had any talent I cannot see how it would have been revealed. I don't recall a single artist was ever mentioned...' HMI found many schools where, typically 'art failed to make much impact on the life of the school', and art rooms which were 'dirty, ill-decorated and utterly lacking in taste or interest'. In one London school the subject was so badly taught that HMI recommended that it should simply be deleted from the curriculum. In a North Riding grammar school HMI added a confidential addendum to the report noting that 'the Art teacher does not know the first thing about art education'.

Whilst many of the correspondents remember practical subjects like woodwork and metalwork with pleasure and took pride in what they created, a number, including Keith Williams, recall the boredom of simple repetitive tasks such as continually planing wood. HMI visited many schools where pupils were neither challenged nor enthused. In a Bradford secondary modern, no acceptable work was seen in woodwork in three of the four years, whilst inspectors were shocked by another school where the teacher's absence on a course meant no woodwork at all had been taught for a year. The girls' practical subjects, domestic science and needlework, were often much better taught and in one school the chair of governors even asked the intriguing question, sadly left unanswered, 'Is it usual for the domestic science mistress to be such a power in the school?'

Comparing the teaching and learning of modern languages in the 50s with that in the last few decades prompts considerable argument. Traditionalists point to the perceived high standard of written translation, especially from English into the foreign language, which was nearly always French, in the past. Others emphasise the weakness of spoken language in the past compared with now.

In the 50s HMI had serious doubts about what seemed an almost wilful determination on the part of some teachers not to use the spoken language. In one Yorkshire grammar school, 'the master, of French birth, makes little of his initial advantage as little French is heard in the classroom', whilst intonation at a boys' grammar school in Surrey was 'poor and indistinct'. A correspondent at a north London grammar school, despite having gone to the school with the prime objective of learning foreign languages, recalls no French oral teaching at all until shortly before the examination in the fifth form. However, it is not clear that even the standard of written French was always as high as often believed and as O-level question papers of the time suggest. The following HMI reports are typical:

> 'Even in the fifth year many pupils find difficulty in using the past tense in simple answers...persistence of elementary errors (i.e. in written work) is marked.' (Bristol grammar school, February 1960)

> 'The boys write a good deal of nonsense... much of which goes uncorrected.' (Sheffield grammar school, February 1956)

> 'Written exercises give an illusory impression of understanding.' (Surrey girls' grammar school, July 1960)

and most tellingly

> 'Pupils... struggle hopelessly with prose composition instead of acquiring the speaking and listening knowledge within their grasp.' (Essex grammar school, May 1956)

Most secondary modern schools hardly taught languages at all and it was not unknown for HMI to recommend that the subject should be simply dropped from the timetable as happened in two Leeds schools, where it was having little impact.

The narrator in a Channel 4 programme, *That'll Teach 'Em*, which reconstructed a 1950s style grammar school for modern teenagers, suggested that PE and games were a huge and successful part of all school life at the time. In many schools this was certainly true and male correspondents, at least, often recall this aspect of their school days with affection. Mike Walmsley recalled his Catholic grammar school in Leeds turning out *twenty* cricket teams each Saturday although Michael Kerrigan, who was at the same school, agreed that 'we played loads of football and cricket on Saturday mornings' but adds 'games were not taught.'

But HMI reports of the time describe less satisfactory situations, including those of numerous girls' schools. A London girls' secondary modern had no qualified PE mistress and so no games at all were played against other schools. Girls' PE was frequently condemned as 'poor', 'weak' or 'barely satis-factory' and HMI often commented on the apathy of older girls towards the subject. In one girls' school the inspector observing a gymnastics lesson insisted that the activity should be stopped immediately on the grounds of safety. The Hampshire boys' grammar school where, in May 1957, 'organised PE has occupied an almost negligible place in the school curriculum' hardly matches the reminiscences of Channel 4. In a Middlesex boys' secondary modern where, in an aside of dubious relevance, HMI noted that the head of department was trained in Germany, 'standards of gymnastics were poor and the pace of lessons slow'. Far-flung pitches and lack of transport to reach them often made a mockery of schedules. In a Liverpool secondary modern whose football pitches were five miles away, PE 'made no positive contri-bution at all to school life'. Keith Williams recalls his school's pitches as half an hour's walk away in each direction. Once time for changing was taken out of the 90-minute period, only twenty minutes was left for games – although it might be argued that even the walk would benefit some children today.

Today the importance of the quality of leadership, especially of the head, governors and senior staff, is seen as crucial to the success of schools. HMI in the 50s also viewed leadership as important and often commented enthu-siastically on inspirational leadership. In a North Riding secondary modern in 1952 not only had the 'ability of the head established a well-run and success-ful school' but he played a major role in the teaching of both maths and English!

Nonetheless, as with teachers, the worst heads were totally unfitted for their task, some appearing to lack any humanity or empathy. Len Privett recalled the second headteacher he worked for as a 'complete tyrant' whilst Ed Adams recounted a 'welcome' to a Leeds secondary modern by the head which hopefully would not happen today:

> .... the door was opened by a small stocky man who eyed me critically over his half-moon glasses as I introduced myself. He took out a turnip watch and indicating an open exercise book told me to sign in at 8.42 am.

Later the head entered the staff room and without a word of welcome to the staff, after a six week break, read out a list of names, room numbers and forms and promptly exited. When Ed, whose classroom was entirely devoid of furni-ture, asked him about textbooks, a syllabus or schemes of work, he replied, 'Yes, yes, we've been going to do something about that this year. You've been to college haven't you?'

Poet Roger McGough recalled an incident involving the head of his grammar school (McGough, 2005 p51). McGough, along with several classmates in the lower sixth, had re-taken O-level maths and Latin in November and was anxiously awaiting the results. The head entered the classroom and told the boys who had re-sat to stand up. Grim-faced, he announced that he had bad news; they had all failed both subjects. The boys slumped in despair. After a pause he told them that he had only been joking and that they had actually all passed both subjects. Finally, after general rejoicing and relief, he turned to one boy and said, 'Except you, you really did fail both'.

A retired Northumberland adviser, Roy Berill, has an explanation for the appointment of the worst heads at the time: the unwillingness of many governors, normally untrained, to accept any professional advice during interviews. With one headship appointment, he tells how governors were unable to choose between two clearly outstanding candidates. To his astonishment one governor suggested that as a compromise they should pick the third candidate whom every one, including the governor making the proposal, had no doubt was far weaker than the other two. Despite Roy's horrified protests the other governors accepted the idea and appointed the third candidate who turned out to be a disaster.

In the 50s HMI were frequently irritated by the poor standard of governors in schools and made their feelings clear in the minutes of post-inspection meetings with governors. At a Devon secondary school, 'the age of the chairman, his deafness and failing memory, combined with his refusal to face up to the needs of a changing educational world, proved insuperable obstacles at such a meeting' (February 1959). At a Liverpool school another governor, also very elderly, made a 'number of comments which neither the Chairman nor HMI could understand so were passed over in silence' (February 1956). Governors often asked inspectors questions whose answers they might have been expected to know themselves. In one school a governor asked HMI why the head was so severe with girls. The reporting inspector suggested, hopefully humorously, that it might be due to the fact the senior mistress was a 'militant feminist'!

Some heads in the past were also startlingly incompetent. It is difficult to imagine many headteachers today going on holiday for the whole six week summer break as did one head early in my career. It is even less likely that they would ask for all the school post for the entire summer to be re-directed to their holiday address. Unfortunately, this head had forgotten that examination results are addressed personally. In mid-August, a number of us arrived at school, eager to distribute A-level results to anxious sixth formers, to find that all the results had been efficiently dispatched by the Royal Mail to an address overseas. In the absence of email or fax machines, only a high-speed race along the M62 by two colleagues to the offices of the Joint Matriculation Board averted complete disaster.

Good teaching and leadership are critical to the success of any school. Today emphasis is placed on outcomes, particularly test and examination results, in judging the effectiveness of schools. How high achievements really were in the past can only be fully understood from the scrutiny of the examination results and what examiners thought of the candidates' efforts.

5

The gold standard in the golden age

One modern myth maintains that the change to the comprehensive system after the mid-60s resulted from the scheming of a few malcontents in the Labour party and university departments of education. In fact, under-achievement in secondary schools was widely recognised as a national embarrassment long before Labour regained power in October 1964. Conservative governments commissioned no fewer than four major reports by the Ministry of Education in 1954, Crowther in 1959, Newsom in 1963 and Beloe in 1965 all considering the same broad issue, the wastage of talent in state schools under the selective system. At the time few doubted the extent of the problem. The *Daily Mirror* stated that 'Britain is letting her teenagers down' and the Times that 'a scandalous waste of talent persists' (Davis, 1990 pp95, 98).

Though these comments referred particularly to the 80 per cent or so of children who did not attend grammar school, the reality was even worse. Analysis of examination statistics of the time reveals a sorry state, even within what is believed now to have been a thriving academic sector. While experts like Newsom concentrated on under-achievement in secondary modern schools, there were also doubts about the performance of grammar schools, particularly in meeting the needs of pupils in the bottom half of the intake. G.H. Bantock, a strong supporter of grammar schools, stressed the need for these schools 'to pay more and a different sort of attention to (the) lower streams' (Bantock, 1963 p118). Since most grammar schools were only three-form entry, the lower streams represented at least one third of the intake. In reality, analysis of examination figures reveal that under-achievement penetrated deeper than one third.

According to the Crowther report in the late 50s a staggering 38 per cent of grammar school pupils failed to achieve more than three passes at O-level (Crowther, 1959 vol. II p203). It is clear that of the entire cohort of 16 year-olds at this time, only about 9 per cent achieved five or more O-levels and that less than half of those who attended grammar schools reached this benchmark. These figures are national averages and include high-achieving direct grant schools like Manchester, Leeds and Bradford Grammar Schools whose results are wrongly portrayed by advocates of a return to selection as typical of all grammar schools then.

The claim in the *Sunday Times* that grammar schools were 'wonderfully successful' (20/08/06), though now widely believed, is not supported by the evidence. It is significant that the same teachers who over-estimated the percentage of schools failed by Ofsted today (chapter 1, p5), also believed the proportion of 16 year-olds passing five O-levels around 1960 to be four times higher than it actually was.

The results of individual schools, although difficult to obtain, are revealing. 'Hightown Grammar' (a pseudonym) in the north west, was researched by C.Lacey. The school had an above average academic intake even amongst local grammar schools. But between 1962 and 1965 only 51 per cent of pupils gained five O-levels, whilst amongst children from working class families the figure was 37 per cent. (Lacey, 1970 p30). Almost a quarter of working-class children left Hightown with no passes at all.

These were the offspring of the most ambitious and determined workers in the town: even assuming few expected their children to stay on to sixth form, surely they must have hoped for greater success than this at O-level?

Not that they did stay on to sixth form: according to Crowther only 10 per cent of 17 year-olds were in full-time education (Crowther, 1959 vol I p6) and even in grammar schools only a third stayed on, many retaking O-levels rather than starting A-level courses. Crowther insisted that 'with few exceptions' all grammar school children should be staying on until they were 18. (vol. 1 p200) The Ministry of Education commissioned an enquiry entitled *Early Leaving* in 1954 from which the figures below have been obtained .

Table 3: Percentage of grammar school pupils achieving no O-level passes: 1954.

All pupils	19%
All working class pupils	24%
All unskilled working class pupils	40%

(Ministry of Education, 1954 p79)

Even amongst the brightest third of grammar school pupils, a third of children from the poorest backgrounds and 17 per cent of all working class children left without a single pass: of nearly 9000 children whose progress was followed up for the report only 23 from unskilled backgrounds ended up with two A-levels.

Some didn't even stay until 15. Howard Parker researched the lives of teenage boys in a tough part of Liverpool in the early 70s and he found that whilst seven of his group had passed the 11+, five had left grammar school before the end of the third year, one lasting less than a year (Parker, 1974 p196). None had left as a result of family financial pressures. Twenty years before *Early Leaving* (p88) had confirmed that financial considerations were a factor in only 15 per cent of the decisions to leave early. More importantly, according to Parker, 'they felt uneasy and out of place at grammar school and resented their treatment there', including derogatory references by staff to their home district. Roy Hattersley also believed that every child at his Sheffield grammar school, in the early 50s, should have been a candidate for 'a long striped scarf' (i.e. university) but too often the school's 'determination to distinguish sheep from goats.... convinced children of real ability that higher education was beyond their talents' (Hattersley, 1983 p207).

The Hightown figures, above, are not untypical. HMI gave a detailed breakdown of the performance of a boys' grammar school in a prosperous part of Dorset in November 1959. Fourteen per cent had left after the fourth year having taken no public exams and a further 14 per cent failed to achieve any O-level passes in the fifth year. So nearly 30 per cent left with no O-level passes. Only 38 per cent in total achieved 5 passes and whilst most of these stayed on into the sixth form, less than a third of them (i.e. about 13 per cent of the total intake) had gained two A-level passes by the end. The school didn't impress HMI, the history inspector noting dryly that for most pupils the 'latest authenticated news was that Queen Anne was dead'.

But another Dorset grammar school, which selected the brightest 17 per cent of local boys, was thought to be a 'good' school in May 1956 even though 34 per cent of pupils left without even attempting O-level. The head commented with calm indifference that some boys 'will always find the challenge of the grammar school too much'. The senior inspector retorted that one third was hardly an insignificant proportion! Results earlier in the 50s were even worse. When Peter Ginns took O-levels at his Leicestershire grammar school in 1954, only 28 boys out of 130 (22 per cent) gained 5 O-levels. He and another boy were the only two to pass nine subjects.

Detailed results were analysed for one school for the years 1957 to 1961. The school took in the brightest Roman Catholic boys from a huge area: the entire city of Sheffield, the towns of Barnsley, Chesterfield, Doncaster and Rotherham, large areas of Derbyshire, Nottinghamshire and even part of Lincolnshire. Its catchment area covered those of at least seven Catholic comprehensive schools today. The school was well-regarded. According to HMI in 1956 'those in charge of the school were to be congratulated for having put their house in order'.

Between 1957 and 1961, 454 pupils were successful at O-level, of whom 40 per cent passed five or more subjects. The average number of passes for all pupils was just over four. But differences in achievement between the various streams were vast. The school ran four streams in the O-level year: 5A, 5B, 5C and Upper 4, an express form who took the exams a year early. Of 219 boys in the 5A and U4 streams 72 per cent (157) obtained five O-levels. The picture was very different in the B and C streams which because the U4 class was much smaller than the others included well over half the total intake. In the B streams only 33 per cent passed five subjects, whilst in the C stream over a five year period only two pupils got five passes! The average for the whole of the bottom stream was fewer than two passes per boy.

When compared with modern examination and test data, these figures do not reflect the true position. For although there are figures for examination passes there is no information about boys who left early without sitting examinations or those who sat for but passed no exams.

Nor do these results for individual subjects support familiar arguments for the selective system. Only 15 per cent of pupils passed all three main sciences, often cited as strength of grammar schools, between 1959 and 1961. Only 39 per cent of pupils passed a modern foreign language.

The situation with maths in girls schools has already been discussed but results from individual schools can still shock. In one Yorkshire grammar school fewer than 10 per cent of girls passed maths O-level between 1952 and 1954, excluding those who left before the fifth form. HMI reports refer frequently to the disappointingly small numbers even entered for examinations. In a Cheshire grammar school, only four pupils were studying maths at A-level, 'two of whom are clearly out of their depth' .

A key factor in the small numbers of pupils achieving success at O- and A-level nationally were the low pass rates. Ironically, schools today are criticised because too few students reach the 'expected' standard of five higher passes at GCSE or in maths and English. And yet the high failure rate in the selective 1950s is cited as proof of rigorous standards of education! As examinations were taken by only the brightest 20 per cent or so of the age group, pass rates of less than 60 per cent in most subjects at O-level cannot possibly be an endorsement of contemporary standards. HMI certainly did not see the low figures taking examinations, let alone passing, as evidence of high achievement.

This argument is reinforced by scrutiny of the actual numbers passing individual subjects. The Joint Matriculation Board, then the largest examination board, covered an enormous proportion of England from the Scottish border to the Midlands, including most of the largest cities in the country outside London: Birmingham, Manchester, Liverpool, Leeds, Sheffield and Newcastle. For an area with such a huge population, the total number of pupils passing the major subjects was noticeably low.

Table 4 : Joint Matriculation Board Examination Passes:1958

Subject	O-level		A-level
English language	30468	English	3862
English literature	19599		
Maths	22976		3138
Biology, Chemistry & Physics	25887		10669
French	19839		2562
History	16000		2827
Art	8791		811

(JMB Annual Report, 1958)

Today emphasis is rightly placed on the need for pupils to achieve success in the core subjects, English, maths and science. But in 1958, 27 per cent of the select group who passed English did not pass maths. Today the gap is far smaller. English literature is often cited as a subject where standards have fallen but it is worth noting that a third of those who passed language did not pass literature. Today the difference is only 12 per cent.

In addition, despite the inevitably large number of multiple entries in the three sciences at O-level, the aggregate number of passes for biology, chemistry and physics is still less than in English and barely more than in maths. This indicates the numbers passing all three sciences must have been very much a minority. The figures for some less popular subjects are also extremely low: only 164 candidates passed A-level Spanish with the JMB.

The small numbers of passes notwithstanding, many modern critics argue that the sheer demands of examinations in the 50s at this time gave them a value which is lacking, at least for the brightest pupils, in the modern system.

This raises the questions of whether examinations from this period were as tough as often assumed and whether valid comparisons are possible between examinations which are separated by over half a century? Many experts in this field argue that they are not and that much of the annual debate over exam standards is a waste of time. Alison Wolf points out that Britain is unique in the industrialised world in its emphasis on the monitoring and maintenance of standards over time. (Wolf in Goldstein and Heath, 2000). Other countries see the main purpose of examinations as simply to select amongst groups of students. And a recent QCA paper adds a further relevant point to the debate: 'each individual attaches different value to each part of a subject' (QCA, 2006 p11).

Certainly some of the claims that examinations have become easier are hardly convincing. The *Daily Telegraph* loves to quote examples of questions previously asked at O-level being set more recently at A-level. However, it is the quality of the answer expected not the formulation of the question, which determines the standards of examinations. When I sat O-level in 1959 exactly the same question on the causes of world war one was set for both O- and A-level history.

Channel 4's *That'll teach 'em* gave modern teenagers in a supposed 1950s grammar school O-level papers from the time and then reported gleefully on their poor performance, compared with their results in GCSE a few weeks later. Although not intended seriously it was nevertheless a dishonest exercise. How many 1950s youngsters sat O-level after only the four weeks preparation the teenagers in the programme had? As Ted Wragg pointed out, was it fair to test modern pupils on imperial measurements which the government had asked schools to stop teaching thirty years before?

A number of my *Saga* correspondents referred to finding modern GCSE and A-level papers easier than those of fifty years ago. But this argument, which is often heard from older people, may ignore what they have learnt since leaving school. I only studied French between 1955 and 1963 but how far is my admittedly mediocre command of French today due to learning at school, rather than the result of the time I have spent in France and French Switzerland since? To argue that I might cope with a French GCSE paper now only as a result of what I learnt fifty years ago is disingenuous.

Examination of JMB O- and A-level papers from the 50s does suggest that some, maths, sciences and translation from English to modern foreign languages, may be harder overall. One correspondent, G.C. Wright from Tadcaster, sent a detailed and well-argued letter suggesting that A-level maths and physics papers were tougher in the past. Against this, however, Ken Boston, chief executive of the QCA and himself a scientist, maintains:

> the physics curriculum has developed so much over the last fifteen years in response to the digital age that anyone of my generation who hasn't kept up with physics would find this year's A-level physics paper almost impossible. (*Observer* 13/08/ 06)

And Peter Knight, Vice Chancellor of the University of Central England takes a similar view on maths

> a great wodge of the material I did at A-level is no longer on the syllabus and rightly so [and] some of the material regarded as degree level in the 60s is now in the A-level syllabus. (*Guardian* 15/08/06)

The argument for falling standards in arts papers such as English language and literature or history is far less convincing. English language O-level papers seemed dull enough at the time and would appear laughable to the same target group today, the brightest 20 per cent. Essay titles from the 1959 paper included 'Pleasures of life in a large town', 'Washing day' and 'Coach tours': hardly demanding stuff which, pace the *Daily Telegraph*, could easily have been given to younger children then or now. Candidates were asked to explain the meaning of 'humility' and' suburban' and show the alternative meanings of words such as 'vice' and 'lap'. Again, is that truly beyond today's brightest 16-year olds? English literature consisted of the study of only three books over two years: a Shakespeare play, a novel and a selection of poetry. The questions were predictable and tested only memory. Typically, candidates were asked to write an account of the source of Pip's great expectations, whilst those who had studied *A Midsummer Night's Dream* had to explain the quarrel between Oberon and Titania.

The most academic schools at the time had little patience with either English paper. A questionnaire sent to over 40 of the most selective grammar schools in 1961 revealed that most felt that O-level English actually hindered their teaching of the subject (NA ED 147/1334).

'Abandon clause analysis' demanded one school '...it bores the brightest and the weakest don't get it.' – the 'weakest', note, in a school taking the most able 8-10 per cent of pupils! Latymer Upper School in Edmonton claimed the London English literature O-level paper was no more than a memory test: 'We don't enter our brightest boys for it, although for the weaker brethren it is easy to pass and gives them another subject.' Manchester Grammar School complained, 'It doesn't take more than the odd voice, if donnishly dogmatic, to give the impression that pupils are reaching university as dumb illiterates.'

Professor Brian Cox, chair of the national curriculum English committee in the 1990s, confirms these views:

> By the time O-level was dropped, it was a discredited examination..its approach to literature was too narrow , asking little but basic comprehension and the study of a few books. (Cox, 1995 p105)

Other subjects were equally unchallenging. JMB geography required an account of the two main economic activities in areas, the names already known to candidates, such as the Yorkshire, Nottinghamshire and Derbyshire coalfields. Questions in history were notoriously repetitive and predictable. The classmate of one friend claimed, with only slight exaggeration, that you could always begin answering the final question on the modern syllabus before you even saw the paper. It always asked for the causes of the first world war!

Nor do we hear of papers, which were, without doubt, less challenging than their modern equivalents, such as art, technology or the oral aspect of foreign languages. The O-level art examination in the 50s, which was a single drawing on a title given out at the start, was a world away from the imaginative, skilled and superbly planned work seen in secondary schools today. One boy at the time only ever drew one subject for two whole years: boxers fighting. He told the class before the examination that he would find a title to fit his picture and began work on his familiar drawing, rather like the first world war essayist, without even bothering to look at the question paper. His classmates were intrigued and as they gazed at the inspiring titles offered by the exam board: 'Holiday Adventure', 'The Gardener', 'The Present' and 'Deserted Village', couldn't see where his battling middleweights would fit in. But there it was: the final title was 'Work in Progress' and he was soon deep into a swinging upper cut striking a stubbly jaw, the referee's arm upraised for the count!

As Michael Kerrigan, retired languages HMI, pointed out:

> In so many subjects (and, indeed, in other aspects of school life), so much wider a range of skills is required now – this is very rarely acknowledged, let alone given due recognition.

But the most unexpected insight into examination standards at this time comes not from question papers or HMI inspections but from the annual reports of examiners in different subjects. Whilst various criticisms would be anticipated, it is surprising, in light of the selective entry to public examinations, how basic are so many of the errors highlighted .

Of course examiners and markers enjoy howlers, which may be untypical of the general standard of papers so whilst some of the errors reported from the top fifth of the ability range may raise eyebrows, it is unfair to draw too many conclusions from them. We learn in 1958 that 'Wordsworth sat on top of a bus on Westminster Bridge and saw the town and cinemas' or hear how 'Sir Bastopol' was the hero of the Battle of Balaclava and even that 'Nelson won the Battle of Waterloo in Egypt'. Candidates had written of such strange phenomena as 'The Celtic Fridge' or 'The Prince Concert'.

However, often the examiners make clear that the errors quoted are typical of many, occasionally of most candidates. In English language O-level in 1956, they complained that

> the meaning of paragraphs is unknown to many, the semi-colon has virtually disappeared and commas are scattered at random. The influence of women's magazines, cheap novelettes and TV is more and more evident.

Even at A-level, taken by only a few thousand of the brightest 18 year-olds across northern England, 'paragraphs are often absent, punctuation poor, commas used instead of full stops and apostrophes unknown'. In the 1960 history O-level exam pupils believed that 'higher' was a verb as in 'the Chancellor 'highered' taxes'. Spelling errors in the 1958 O-level general paper, normally not taken until the sixth form, included 'Brittain', 'deffinate', 'fivety', 'polytitions' and 'Poit Loriet'. Surprisingly, English examiners in 1955 complained of the misuse of 'of' as in 'he should of done it' – a mistake often thought to be of more recent origin.

In 1957, the English language (O-level) report said that some scripts were 'not far removed from illiteracy' whilst in literature examiners bemoaned the total lack of understanding of such simple terms as 'scene', 'passage' or 'incident'. The report ends, 'too many candidates, in fact, were unable to understand the question paper'. That remark sheds light on the modern practice of quoting past question papers in isolation as 'proof' of falling standards.

The poor vocabulary of some candidates is unexpected. The English Language report for the O-level paper in 1959, accepts that words such as 'flaccid', 'panacea' or, interestingly, 'militant' might be too difficult for fifth formers. But the report writer finds it incredible that so many pupils were ignorant of the meaning of 'ludicrous', or 'suburban'.

The picture was similar in other subjects. The A-level maths report in 1960 complained that

> Too many candidates clearly had no understanding of the subject matter of most questions: a depressing feature included the tendency to manipulate symbols without understanding them, to fake results and indulge in ludicrous cancelling .

Examiners do not usually specify the proportion of candidates they are criticising but the 1955 maths O-level report noted that only 25 per cent were able to identify correctly the lowest common multiple of 88 and 112. And the following year history examiners reported that the majority of candidates spelt 'independence' incorrectly, despite the word appearing on the question paper.

Surprisingly, in view of the apparent difficulty of prose translations in modern language papers from this period, references to the most elementary errors in foreign languages abound. The 1956 French O-level report speaks of widespread ignorance of such common words as '*aujourd'hui*', '*demain*', '*maintenant*', '*trop*' and '*bruit*' whilst at A-level, examiners were shocked at the frequent mistranslation of commonplace words such as '*patron*', '*diable*' and '*toucher*'. The small numbers of pupils taking minority languages meant that standards in Russian, Spanish or German were no higher, although the confused soul who translated 'Of course, at that time' into German as '*Naturellement, at das temp*' was hopefully not typical!

Even in physics A-level, often regarded as a subject taken only by the brightest, it is clear that many candidates were hopelessly ill-equipped for the examination's demands. In the report on the 1960 paper the examiners spelt out failings that applied to a large number of candidates: weaknesses in 'basic ideas and fundamental principles', 'answers unrelated to the questions', 'poor presentation' and a 'lack of physical thinking in numerical work'.

Most unexpected, in view of the small percentage of the relevant age groups sitting O- and A-level examinations, is the frequency with which examiners refer to the large number of candidates who should never have been entered for the papers at all. In 1957 the report for A-level English complains of the large number who not only failed but were marked below 20 per cent. A year earlier the same examiners had written of 'the many whose candidature had been a waste of time and money and [who] had clearly never read the books'. For O-level maths in 1956 the report also went beyond the normal list of specific errors to criticise entering candidates 'whose knowledge and understanding were too slight for them to have the slightest chance of passing'. In physics the same year some O-level scripts were 'of an incredibly low standard'.

According to the literature O-level report in 1956, 'sometimes whole groups are entered in which no more than a quarter have any chance of passing'. Note that the examiners stressed that they were not referring to isolated instances. It seems that a quarter of many classes of the brightest youngsters in England should never even have been entered for the exam. Yet how likely is it that if the top set in an average comprehensive school today were to be prepared for a 50s-style O-level literature paper over two years, a quarter of the group would fail? And most modern top sets would contain a wider ability range than the entry for O-level at the time.

The 1950s and early 60s were an age of transition in education and schools had improved significantly since the years before and immediately after the war. Yet to understand properly where schools stand today in terms of pupil achievement it is important to know where they have come from. There was no golden age fifty years ago. Whilst I would not agree with Kathleen Ollerenshaw, the Conservative educationalist from Lancashire who condemned postwar secondary education as a 'disaster' (Jones, 2003 p49), it is evident that deep-seated structural problems remained throughout the period. Working-class children were under-represented in grammar schools, those from the poorest families hardly ventured there at all. Many of those who made it to grammar schools under-achieved. Despite coming from the most able fifth of the population, thousands left at the end of the fourth year without taking any public examinations or after the fifth year with a tiny number of O-levels or none at all.

Above all, under-achievement was rife in secondary modern schools where many repeated work more suitable for the old elementary schools. Even though at least 14 per cent of secondary modern children had been misplaced by the 11+ and should have been in a grammar school, only 4 per cent were ever entered for even one O-level. Although the best schools would have stood out in any age, far too many pupils of all abilities were condemned to boring, undemanding work. In 1961 the Ministry of Education even described the depth of 'concern felt in the Universities of Oxford and Cambridge about... deficiencies in the general education of candidates coming to them from schools' (Ministry of Education 1960-1 p26). Whilst it was a time of re-building, courage and energy for most of the teaching profession, the post-war years offer no blue-print for the future. All the major problems in schools today, with the possible exception of specific behavioural issues, existed then – and often to a far greater extent. Using uncritical nostalgia as a weapon against modern teachers and schools is demoralising and dishonest, particularly when combined with an overly pessimistic view of the present which bears as little relation to reality as the false picture painted of the past.

6

Schools today –
the true picture (1)

Chapter 1 indicated the serious obstacles to school improvement after the war, including the appalling buildings and teacher shortages, which must be taken into account in any assessment of education at that time. Equally, any critic of contemporary education should take account of problems facing schools and teachers today, which either did not exist in the past or were much less extensive. For example, many who contacted me through *Saga magazine* bemoaned the limited horizons presented by many schools, particularly secondary moderns. Yet there were also frequent references to the often smooth transition from school to work, especially for working-class boys. The impact on schools of the de-stabilisation of communities caused by the decline of industries like shipbuilding, mining and steel-making from the 1970s onwards has been considerable. That easy transition to work no longer exists and the task of teachers, particularly those of older pupils, has been made more difficult as a result.

Putnam (2000) and Wilkinson (2005) *inter alia* have demonstrated conclusively that the most serious damage to family life, child health and therefore to educational prospects, comes not from absolute poverty but from relative poverty resulting from inequality. Whilst Britain remains one of the richest countries in the world and inequality has lessened in recent years, it is still less equal than in the 50s and less equal than many other western countries. The PISA programme of the OECD, which compares school systems across the world, has shown that children from single parent families, particularly when poor, are more likely to under-achieve in school. This effect is more marked in the USA and the UK than elsewhere. As with the effect on communities of industrial decline, the rise in the number of single-parent families in recent decades has been significant with numbers doubling between 1986 and 2000 (*The Times*, 27/09/2002).

Any dispassionate observer of Britain's social history would recognise the cultural richness and economic benefits which successive generations of immigrants have brought to this country. However the growth in the numbers of children for whom English is an additional language has presented challenges to schools today which were rarely met in the past. HMI, inspecting an Islington school in the 50s, thought it worthy of comment that 3 per cent of the pupils were non-native English speakers: this represents a quarter of the current average for every single school in the country today.

The increasingly bizarre, as opposed to poor, behaviour of some children, whether linked to family trauma, drugs, diet, psychiatric problems or exposure to violent videos and computer games, has added massively to the pressures on headteachers, teachers, and support staff.

Although less easy to quantify, the extreme reluctance of some parents to accept the authority and expertise of teachers is widely identified as an obstacle to the smooth running of schools. No headteacher would wish to return to an over-deferential age which, at worst, provided a cover for petty tyrants, sadists, even serial abusers. But the time consumed today by a handful of parents, who demand that schools justify every interaction with their child, however petty, is disproportionate.

Yet there is overwhelming evidence that state schools in England are now serving the nation well. Since 1994, Her Majesty's Chief Inspector of Schools (HMCI) has produced an annual report based largely on the inspection reports of up to a quarter of all schools in the country. By 2005, virtually every school had been inspected three times in the previous ten or twelve years. No large industrial country in the world has subjected its schools to closer and more regular scrutiny. Some, like France, have never inspected whole institutions.

Despite well-publicised stories of rogue inspectors, most Ofsted teams lean over backwards to combine fairness to the school with a rigorous examination of its strengths and weaknesses. Ofsted's conclusions about state schools in England have been positive, overwhelmingly so. Yet few would know this from the way its findings are presented in the media. Either editors, columnists and education correspondents believe that Ofsted is inaccurate in its portrayal of state education – in which case why do they regard the criticisms it does make as so authoritative – or they are grossly distorting its findings?

The view taken is unambiguous. The annual report of HMCI for 2004-5, the most recent available at the time of writing, uses a four-point grading system to assess various aspects of a school's performance: *excellent/very good, good, satisfactory* and *unsatisfactory*. The results summarised below are based on the individual reports, lesson observations and close scrutiny of examination and test results for about one in four of all the schools in the country, which amounts to several thousand institutions. This section only deals with academic standards and progress and leadership. Behaviour and other issues will be considered later.

Table 5: Ofsted Evaluation of Schools

Secondary schools	Assessment			
(all figures percentages)	Excellent/Very good.	Good.	Satisfactory.	Unsatisfactory.
Overall effectiveness	26	44	23	7
Improvement since last inspection	22	43	27	9
Educational standards	21	53	19	7
Teaching and learning	22	56	17	5
Leadership of head teachers	62	29	17	4

Primary schools	Assessment			
(all figures percentages)	Excellent/Very good.	Good.	Satisfactory.	Unsatisfactory.
Overall effectiveness	19	49	27	4
Improvement since last inspection	17	45	30	8
Educational standards	16	55	25	5
Teaching and learning	15	59	23	3
Leadership of head teachers	47	38	12	3

(HMCI Annual Report 2004-5)

In the early 90s Michael Barber, later adviser to the Blair government on education, writing at a time when early Ofsted reports indicated higher levels of unsatisfactory teaching than today, quoted teachers' union leaders asking why there was not more emphasis on the majority of lessons which were judged to be at least satisfactory (Barber, 1996 p146). At the time, Barber warned against the complacency implicit in these comments. But must it still be regarded as complacent to expect more emphasis from the media and politicians on the 95 per cent of secondary teaching and 97 per cent of that in primaries which is now satisfactory or better? More teaching is now judged at least good than was graded as at least satisfactory when Barber was writing. In addition, a significant feature of Ofsted's approach, which has received little public attention outside the teaching profession, has been the clearly stated intention, as schools improve, to judge them more severely. 'Satisfactory.' said HMCI David Bell in 2003, 'is no longer good enough' (*The Guardian*, 20/11/03).

Neither the statistics quoted nor Ofsted's readiness to raise its own critical standards suggests a system in crisis. It is true that in 2006 the National Audit Office reported that about 28 per cent of schools were unsatisfactory. (National Audit Office, 2006) But this figure was achieved by aggregating all schools found to be unsatisfactory by Ofsted with the lowest achieving quarter of schools, many of which had been judged as at least satisfactory. John Dunford, General Secretary of the Association of Colleges and School Leaders, noted that there is always going to be a lowest quarter in any rank order, so using the NAO analysis means that a certain number of schools will always be 'failing'. The Public Accounts Committee mounted the same flawed attack on state schools in October 2006. This time schools were defended by both the Prime Minister who commented 'they are changing the definition of what is a failing school to include a whole series of schools that aren't failing', and the *Times Education Supplement* which stated in blunter terms, 'Critics need to get their facts right' (*TES*, 20/10/06).

Further indications of the success of schools come from the views of parents, pupils and teachers. All political parties and much of the media repeatedly stress the key role of parents in driving up standards in schools in the future. In this case why is so little attention paid to parents' views on the current situation in schools? Evidence of parents' opinions is freely available in HMCI's report. A summary of the results of thousands of questionnaires filled out by parents of pupils in schools inspected by Ofsted is as follows:

Table 6: Parents' Views of Schools

Secondary schools	Assessment			
	Excellent/very good.	Good.	Satisfactory.	Unsatisfactory.
(all figures percentages)				
Parents' satisfaction with school	36	44	18	2

Primary schools	Assessment			
	Excellent/very good.	Good.	Satisfactory.	Unsatisfactory.
(all figures percentages)				
Parents' satisfaction with school	49	41	9	1

(HMCI Annual Report, 2004-5)

Chris Woodhead, Michael Barber and others have remarked that some parents will always support their child's school, however poor, and that even the most hopeless schools seem to command a surprising degree of parental confidence. An Ofsted report in 2006 on parental satisfaction appears to confirm this (Ofsted, 2006).

In reality, the figures for parental satisfaction in schools vary significantly according to the quality of the school. Only 11 per cent of parents of children at failing secondary schools believed the school to be good and none thought the school any better than good, compared with the 95 per cent of parents at schools Ofsted judged to be good, who thought that their school was good or better. Polls of parents whose children actually attend state schools show higher levels of satisfaction with the system than polls of the general public. Is this due to loyalty or to first-hand knowledge rather than the result of second hand views influenced by sensational newspaper stories? Research by Professor David James suggests that teachers, governors and other education professionals are more likely to send their children to state schools than other middle class parents. This applies even to those who are wealthy or have been privately educated themselves. 'They have a greater knowledge of the realities of state schooling and fewer irrational fears', says James (*TES*, 13/10/06).

Surveys of teachers also show greater enthusiasm for the profession than often thought. Of course teachers are not starry-eyed. They are tired of bureaucracy, long hours leading to a poor work-life balance, bad pupil behaviour and lack of support when they are newly qualified. Head teachers struggle under the weight of initiative overload and, despite promises of reduction in bureaucracy, a constant stream of questionnaires, forms and demands for information. Even so, research in 2005 for the DfES showed that 90 per cent of teachers found their job interesting and challenging, compared with 77 per cent of graduates in other work (DfES, 2005). Only 7 per cent would choose another profession despite the demands of the job. A survey in 2006 (*TES*, 28/07) also showed that teachers suffered the least boredom of any graduate profession. Even more telling are the results of the *Teach First* programme, designed to give high-flying graduates a taste of teaching in disadvantaged London schools before entering careers in business. Over 90 per cent lasted the full two years and over half actually stayed on in teaching even though most had their first taste of the classroom in schools with above average difficulties. These figures hardly suggest a system in permanent crisis.

There is a lack of balance in comments made about national examination and test results. In part this is caused by confusion over what children should actually achieve at different ages. The DfES talks of 'expected' levels in National Curriculum tests: level 4 for 11 year-olds, level 5 for 14-year olds and five passes at grade C or above at GCSE. The trouble is that nobody has ever agreed on what the term 'expected' really means! The first head of the National Curriculum Council, Duncan Graham, and Professor Paul Black, who pioneered the assessment system, clearly understood it to mean 'average', a straightforward enough concept. But Graham, as Mike Baker, the BBC education correspondent has noted, complained that politicians like Kenneth Clarke demonstrated 'a calculated ignorance of the meaning of averages' and would bemoan the fact that so many children were below average! (Baker, 2005)

Now the DfES claims that at the age of 11 most children are expected to achieve level 4: there is no longer an average at all. As Baker points out: 'Is it really so dreadful that 23 per cent of children fail to reach a standard that only fifteen years ago was regarded as an average?' And even by today's criteria, 'most children' are achieving the expected level. Indeed, if all children with serious special educational needs, for whom English is an additional language or who are discounted through absence are excluded, the total is over 90 per cent. Almost all children who could fairly be expected to reach the 'expected level' already do so.

Furthermore, overall figures continue to rise and results indicate consistent improvement, at all levels. The proportion of 16 year-olds gaining 5 O-levels passes or higher grade GCSEs rose from 22 per cent in 1975 to over 50 per cent by 2000, whilst over the same period the percentage gaining two or more A-level passes increased from 12 per cent to over 20 per cent. At Key Stage 2, the percentage of 11 year-olds reaching the 'expected' level 4 increased from 48 per cent in English in 1995 to 79 per cent in 2005 and in maths from 44 per cent to 75 per cent. Yet this progress is routinely dismissed as the result of the assessment becoming easier and the results are portrayed as being incredible and a consequence of a 'fall' in standards.

Comparisons of testing over time are recognised to be difficult. However, detailed subject by subject research by the Schools Curriculum and Assessment Authority (SCAA, 1996) and its successor, the QCA (QCA, 2005) has not shown evidence of the wholesale slippage in standards which is assumed so readily by critics. Cambridge Assessment, one of the most authoritative bodies in this field in Europe, has looked at standards over time in both KS2 and KS4 English. It found that 'the experimental evidence from all subjects and key stages indicated that there has been a substantial real improvement in children's achievement' (Massey, 2005 p5). Although they believed that national tests had exaggerated the extent of the improvement, which was the only part of the report seized on by some critics, there had still been 'significant gains in achievement'

Professor Peter Tymms agrees with Cambridge Assessment that improvements in primary test results in recent years do not simply reflect a rise in standards but result in part from better preparation in test techniques so that teachers are teaching to the test (Tymms *et al*, 2005). But reporting of Tymms' findings often fails to mention that he accepts there has been a real rise in standards, not the fall so often implied.

A detailed comparison by Cambridge Assessment of GCSE English scripts of 2004 with those of 1993 and 1994 and with O-level in 1980 showed no evidence of a decline in standards, rather the reverse (Massey *et al*, 2005). Whilst spelling was better in 1980 than in either the 90s or in 2004,in other respects such as writing, vocabulary and punctuation, the scripts of 2004 were better than those of 1993 and 1994 and as good if not better than those of 1980 when fewer pupils took the examination. Significantly, the improvements had taken place at all levels, not just amongst the brightest pupils.

Even if the critics are correct and examinations have become easier, this does not prove that overall standards have dropped. It is necessary to determine by how much the standard has fallen in relation to both the increase in pass rates and the numbers taking the examination. If a GCSE grade C is really easier to obtain today than a pass at O-level was in 1960, is it twice, three or four times as easy? A threefold difference seems impossible. It would imply that a modern student who achieves 75 per cent at GCSE, if well prepared over two years for the O-level examination would only gain 25 per cent.

Yet the number of students achieving five or more GCSEs at grade C or better is now between six and seven times the number getting five O-levels before the spread of comprehensive education. This improvement cannot possibly be explained away by any 'lowering' of the standard of the examination. The point applies as strongly to A-level and even more to minimal qualifications. Over 80 per cent of the most elderly members of the population, those in their mid-80s and older, have no educational qualification, compared with only around 5 per cent of those leaving school today.

These figures show up the shallowness of the 'more means worse' argument. It may well be plausible that the average standard of entrants for GCSE, A-level or degree finals is lower than in the past, when a far smaller proportion of the relevant age group took these examinations. The proportion of 18 year-olds going to university today is around six times larger than in 1960. There is no evidence that the entire cohort forty years were better prepared for degree courses than the brightest sixth of university entrants today. If so, why did so many Oxford and Cambridge graduates end up with third class degrees in the 50s and 60s – surely they weren't all rowing or performing with Footlights?

Critics of modern examination standards also ignore the increases in the number of examinations entered. The current key government benchmark only considers those achieving five higher grade GCSEs, whereas in comprehensive schools today most pupils take eight or nine subjects. In the 50s even the select group who took O-level sat, on average, fewer than five subjects each. The argument which judges educational standards only by the depth of the study concerned and ignores breadth totally is false. For example, when the Higginson Report, published in 1988, recommended broadening A-level to five subjects from three, critics, including Margaret Thatcher, universally assumed that this implied a lowering of standards. Obviously each separate subject might have been studied to a lower level than before. Why, though, should the overall educational standard achieved by the student drop if he or she studies five subjects to 60 per cent of the level to which three were taken previously?

And if improvements in results are due to papers getting easier, why have they become so much easier for girls, whose results have improved so markedly over the past forty years? The suggestion that they prefer coursework is irrelevant since their improvement has been as great in papers without it. This change alone points towards a more complex explanation than papers becoming easier. Whilst teaching has greatly improved, a key factor has been the increased pressure on students, parents and teachers for examination success. Pupils' awareness of the significance of exams for their future, as well as the quality of their preparation for them is of a totally different order than even twenty years ago. Front page photographs of tearful girls hugging each other on results days, sophisticated revision guides, study days and after-school coursework clubs all drive home a relentless message: examinations matter.

Whilst the earlier story of examination results being thoughtlessly re-directed to a holiday address is hardly typical, a casual lack of preparedness for examinations in the past, including the wrong choice of books or entire syllabuses, was not uncommon. Several correspondents related alarming stories. Jackie Scott-Mandeville was taught completely the wrong syllabus in economics at a prestigious Hertfordshire grammar school in the mid-60s: the whole group failed and it cost her a university place. Anne Pugh's class at a 'very good' co-educational grammar school in Worcestershire studied the wrong text for A-level German for two years without the teacher realising.

It seems likely that the greater stress placed on examinations partly explains the improvement in girls' results. There is abundant evidence that teenage girls take a more considered view of their future options than most boys of the same age so they responded more positively to the increased profile of public examinations.

The full implications of the changed structure of exams, particularly at A-level, are also misunderstood. Critics ask how examinations could not have become easier when percentage pass rates have risen to the high 90s, compared with the mid-70s which were the norm twenty years ago. But today's students, taking six different examinations as part of a modular course, already know over 80 per cent of their final mark before they even sit the final examination. Those heading for failure usually drop the subject concerned or defer until the following year. This, allied to better teacher assessment and syllabus knowledge, means that students are aware of the exact level they have reached in the subject, compared with the past when so many sailed blithely towards disappointment in late August. Dr.Mike Cresswell, director-general of the AQA examination board also points out that '... the increase in the number of students awarded an A grade is only equivalent to one or two students getting the top grade in an average school or college' (*The Guardian*, 15/08/06).

On the other hand, Professor Tymms offers hard evidence from the ALIS project at Durham University suggesting there has been grade inflation at A-level, with a large increase in students getting A grades, from 13 per cent in 1992 to nearly 24 per cent in 2005 (Tymms *et al*, 2005). It seems unlikely that such a significant increase is the result of a growth in the numbers of very bright youngsters. Nevertheless, improved examination technique, teachers with better subject knowledge and more informed decisions on entry have led to a sharp reduction in the number of the lowest grades (E, N (now defunct) and U) being awarded. These fell by a third from 1992 to 2001.

Feedback from teachers on how pupils can do better has improved enormously even in the past decade or so and the weakest students have benefited most. The reduction in the lowest grades – not the increase in high grades – has been the single biggest numerical change at both A-level and GCSE. This is what has helped to push up the proportion of higher grades. It is significant that whilst at A-level, grade As increased by 50 per cent in the 1990s as a percentage of *all* entries, the increase when only grades A-D are considered was less than half that. There has been a similar pattern at GCSE.

Finally, as John Gray points out, the social composition of the pupil population has changed as better-educated parents have created higher expectations (Gray in Goldstein and Heath, 2000). International studies have demonstrated that one of the biggest single determinants of a child's success at school is the educational level attained by the mother, especially in higher secondary education (A-level). The percentage of girls achieving A-level rose almost 400 per cent from the cohort born in the 1940s to those born in the 1960s, most of whom were the products of comprehensive education. The latter group are now in their mid-thirties to mid-forties, many with children at or approaching GCSE or A-level age. In the light of this, why is it so surprising that there has been an explosion both in the numbers taking public examinations and of those achieving higher grades? Despite all the allegations of deliberately lowered standards, the improvement was predictable.

The improvement in examination results apart, the breadth of the curriculum has increased greatly. As noted earlier, in the past it was common to drop subjects now part of the core curriculum. Even in the 1980s the curriculum for pupils in the fourth and fifth years often constrained future career choices with some girls studying little beyond typing, office studies and child care, with no clear educational progression. This wholesale closing down of opportunities has been reduced by the national curriculum.

Many of the more general criticisms of state education today are characterised by inaccuracy and sloppy thinking. There is the misuse of statistics which are frequently misreported or misinterpreted. Perhaps the most notorious example was Kenneth Clarke's' assertion, after the first KS2 tests for 7 year-olds in 1992, that 28 per cent of the age group could not distinguish the first three letters of the alphabet. Had someone misplaced a decimal point? The true figure, revealed a few days later, was closer to 2.8 per cent! By then it was too late to remedy the damage done to the nation's primary schools and their teachers by the critical news stories and broadcast comments. The eventual retraction was largely ignored by the media (Gipps, 1993 p31).

More serious, and still widely disseminated, is the mistaken assertion that 'a quarter of children leave primary school unable to read or write'. Every commentator, including the Prime Minister, has used this 'fact' to attack schools in the past few years. It would be hard to find a reputable national newspaper or political periodical in the country which has not discussed the implications of this educational 'failure'. *The Economist* of January 28th 2006 stated that a quarter of children leave primary school 'without being able to read or write'. The charge is based on the statistic that 21 per cent (not a quarter) of children fail to achieve level 4 in English tests. Level 4 is the 'expected' level, a term which itself raises questions already debated. It seems that no one, including Tony Blair, who has quoted this 'fact', has actually read the description of level 3, which is achieved by most children who fail to reach level 4.

Pupils at level 3 in reading are said by the QCA, which is responsible for the testing and marking of all National Curriculum tests, 'to read a variety of texts fluently and accurately. They read independently, using strategies appropriately to establish meaning'. The writing of level 3 pupils is

> often organised, imaginative and clear. The basic grammatical structure of sentences is usually correct... Spelling and punctuation [are] usually accurate. Handwriting is joined and legible.

Jo Hussey from Croydon quoted briefly from the writing of an 'illiterate' pupil who only attained level 3 (*TES*, 11/08/06) 'Nonchalant is how I would describe her... [and later]... he felt the wrath of my mum as she loomed over him' He also used the word 'surreptitious' correctly. Level 3 is certainly not an ideal level for an 11 year-old to have reached and many may struggle with aspects of the secondary curriculum. However, nearly 40 per cent catch up with the 'expected' level by the age of 14.

The description of level 3 and the example given by Jo Hussey could not reasonably be described as indications of illiteracy. And it is clear from correspondence to the press or on websites that many people interpret the failure to achieve level 4 as an indication of illiteracy in the most elementary Victorian sense, the inability to read or write more than one's name.

Sir Digby Jones, former Director-General of the CBI, made even more sweeping claims. In a speech in August 2005 he assumed that any pupil who did not achieve a Grade C in English or maths at GCSE was 'unable to read, write or add up properly' (*The Times*, 26/08/05). This doubled the already fictitious figure of 25 per cent illiterates. He also suggested that achieving the equivalent of a GCSE grade C was 'regarded as fundamental right for all in the 20th century' though he was not clear about when this was the case. Writing in the *Sunday Times* (22/07/06), Minnette Marrin also mistakenly assumed that all those who fail to achieve a grade C in English are 'functionally illiterate'. This is a complete misinterpretation of the term. Tom Sticht, who has worked as a consultant on literacy issues for over thirty years, wrote in 2005 that since he began his work on the topic, the number of so-called illiterates in the country had supposedly risen thirteen times. According to some reports, it now embraced 80 per cent of the population! He looked forward, he said, to 'getting 100 per cent of adults declared functionally illiterate!' (Sticht, 2005).

This casual misuse of statistics is not confined to prime ministers, business leaders and columnists. In the mid-90s Chris Woodhead, then HMCI, famously claimed that 15,000 teachers in England and Wales were incompetent. The sole basis for the statement was that Ofsted observations indicated that 3 per cent of lessons were unsatisfactory. The figure of 15,000 represented 3 per cent of the total number of serving teachers at the time. But Ofsted only monitored teachers briefly every four and kept no data on individuals. The figure could have resulted just as plausibly from *all* teachers teaching 3 per cent of their lessons unsatisfactorily as 15,000 teaching all theirs badly! However, Woodhead's interpretation made much better headlines!

In his 2002 book *Class War* it is twice claimed that the leadership of nearly a third of head teachers is unsatisfactory (Woodhead, 2002 pp35, 85). What is the source for such a figure? Certainly not the annual report of HMCI. In the three years before the book was published these reports, of which two were written when Chris Woodhead was chief inspector, showed unsatisfactory leadership and management to be as follows:

Table 7: Percentage of unsatisfactory leadership and management in schools

Year	Secondary	Primary
2000/1	5	7
1999/00	11	10
1998/9	8	11

(HMCI Annual Reports)

The most recent available report, for 2004/05, shows leadership to be inadequate in 3 per cent of primary schools and 4 per cent of secondary schools. In his last annual report before *Class War* was published (2000/1), HMCI, said that the quality of secondary leadership and management 'is improving generally: the proportion of schools where (it is) very good or better has increased while the proportion where it is poor has been halved'. Noting the 'challenging and increasingly complex role of primary head teachers', he reported that the quality of leadership and management in primary schools had improved 'even when set against changing demands'. Why are such errors accepted so uncritically by the media, when only a few moments spent checking would reveal the truth?

A further flaw in much of the criticism of state schools is gross exaggeration of the extent of approaches to teaching which are associated by critics with egalitarianism and left-wing ideology. Woodhead claims that in '1969 teaching was a subversive activity. The idea that a school might be an institution dedicated to the pursuit of knowledge was passé' (Woodhead, 2002 p42). What nonsense! The vast majority of teachers then, as now, were concerned to help their pupils gain the knowledge and skills to achieve the best qualifications possible and to lead happy, fulfilled lives.

Other targets for similarly over-heated comments are mixed-ability and group teaching. In reality, practically all head teachers approach the question of mixed-ability teaching versus setting by ability pragmatically. The issue is rarely clear cut and varies from subject to subject. There are inherent difficulties with setting. There is the danger of teachers holding low expectations of pupils and of children being placed in the wrong sets, as well as the false assumption by some staff that it removes the need to differentiate amongst pupils.

Yet, these caveats bear no relation to Ferdinand Mount's patronising generalisation that there is 'no need for comprehensive schools to abandon competitive testing or streaming', as if all comprehensive schools were wedded only to mixed ability. (Mount, 2004 p277) Melanie Philips says that 'Crosland's (Minister of Education in the 60s) intention to preserve streaming in comprehensive schools lost out to mixed ability classes' (Philips, 1996 p277) whilst Woodhead claims that 'a genuine comprehensive would not, according to the purist orthodoxy of the day, contemplate setting or streaming' (Woodhead, 2002 p.45).

Caroline Benn's research, however, based on HMI reports, showed that even in 1968 only 4 per cent of comprehensive schools organised teaching on fully mixed-ability lines even in the first year [year 7] (Benn and Chitty, 1997 p251). In the mid-70s HMI reported that only 2 per cent of comprehensive schools taught mixed ability classes in all five years and even in London the figure was only 7 per cent (Benn and Chitty, p251). Studies in the 1980s found 80 per cent of comprehensive schools set for maths after the first year and 93 per cent after the second (Cockcroft, 1982). Whatever the arguments for and against mixed ability-teaching, this totally refutes the image of a widespread, ideologically based commitment to it in comprehensive schools.

My survey for this book of members of the Council of the Association of College and School Leaders, all headteachers or senior staff with vast collective experience in their own and other schools, revealed that not one of them had come across a comprehensive school ideologically opposed to setting by ability. It is true that recent figures from the DfES have shown that less than half of comprehensive schools classes are set, a figure seized on by some, including David Cameron, when he was Conservative education spokesman, to resurrect old arguments. The misinterpretation of this figure reveals how seriously the reporting of educational issues is distorted and misrepresented because of the ignorance of journalists and politicians about school organisation.

Many schools which have no objection on principle to setting – including the one of which I was head – leave it to the end of year 7 so that pupils can settle in. This is understandable and hardly indicative of zealous egalitarianism. Few schools set in areas such as PE, technology, art or personal, social and health education – subjects which people outside schools would never expect to be organised by ability. There are certain optional subjects in Years 10 and 11 such as music or a minority language which may produce only one group, particularly in small schools, which prevents setting. The DfES figure quoted is, therefore, not nearly as low as it first appears.

The debate over primary pupils working in groups, as opposed to whole class teaching, is equally clouded by misinformation. Critics claim correctly that at worst group work can lead to aimless activity, lacking structured learning. The same criticism can be levelled at poor whole-class teaching where children switch off as the teacher talks incessantly. In reality, however, as with mixed-ability teaching in secondary schools, group teaching never dominated the primary classroom in the manner portrayed. Studies by Maurice Galton, Peter Mortimore and others in the late 80s showed at least twice as much time was spent on whole class teaching as on group work (Galton, 1995 p11).

The teaching of English has long been a favourite target of criticism. Professor Brian Cox was one of the authors of the *Black Papers* in the late 1960s, which attacked so-called progressive methods in education. But later, as chair of the English working group which reviewed the early National Curriculum, he was appalled by the misuse of evidence and wild generalisations about English teaching by critics who had the support of the then Secretary of State for Education, John Patten. Professor Cox pointed out that, contrary to the claims constantly made, more students were studying Shakespeare and watching live productions of his plays than at any time in the past. In addition, a wide range of pre-nineteenth century texts were taught and teachers at all levels regarded the teaching of grammar, punctuation and sentence construction as a key responsibility. In primary schools phonics was the activity pupils experienced most in learning to read (Cox, 1995 p32).

A regular ploy of school critics is to portray the worst as typical of all. Melanie Philips, the *Daily Mail* columnist, favours this misleading technique. In her book *All Must have Prizes* she quotes a further education lecturer claiming that whilst her current students were at school,

> ..they've never had homework. Their teachers have rarely corrected their work. I really have no idea what they spend their time teaching them in school. None of the teachers seem to know anything. (Phillips, 1996 p28)

Even if these statements are correct, which is questionable, they bear no relation to the picture presented over many years by Ofsted inspections, HMI reports, comparative international studies, examination and test results and school case studies as well as thousands of questionnaires, surveys and interviews with parents, pupils and teachers. All this material is freely available. Ms. Phillips is happy to ignore this huge body of evidence and accept the word of one lecturer describing at second hand the alleged experiences of a handful of students! Similarly, she quotes Chris Woodhead as having met a headteacher, who believed history and English Literature should not be taught at all in schools (Phillips, 1996 p62). This unlikely figure is wholly untypical of heads in this country.

In the early 90s, I welcomed a Conservative MP to my school. The visit was highly revealing about the influence of critics of education at the time. He seemed surprised at the most commonplace aspects of school life. The pupils did homework! We set internal examinations! Parents received regular reports! We played games against other schools! When I pointed out to him that he would find all local schools very similar in these respects, he looked incredulous. Yet I had visited these schools and had seen the evidence at first hand.

At their worst, attacks on state education are as confused as they are inaccurate. Melanie Phillips claims that GCSE is 'the examination that quintessentially offered prizes to all' (Phillips, 1996 p333). The implication is that all pupils at GCSE gain 'prizes' of equal worth. Yet only 3 per cent of entries receive the top A* grade: the proportion of students is even less as a single candidate may gain several A*s. On the other hand, we are constantly told that only the higher grades above C are worth anything and it is disgraceful that 'only' 50 per cent of youngsters achieve five or more higher passes. Is the system guilty of giving away too many or too few prizes? Her criticism is contradictory.

When attacks involve what should be taught, the fog thickens. David Cameron demanded that children should be taught about 'what Henry VIII did' and not about 'his marital difficulties'. (*Daily Telegraph*, 27/07/05). Really? Henry's marital difficulties led to the execution of two queens, the divorce of two more and the creation of the Anglican church. They influenced this country's political, diplomatic, military and social history for nearly three hundred years. In the early 90s Sheila Lawlor wrote in a pamphlet for the Centre of Policy Studies, that children aged 8 should be made to learn the rhyme 'I had a little nut tree' by heart. I wrote to her pointing out that one of my children, then aged 8, was reading *Great Expectations* each evening and might look slightly askance at being asked to re-learn a nursery rhyme. Not that 'I had a little nut tree' would be acceptable now. It's about Henry VIII's marital difficulties.

7

Schools today –
the true picture (2)

N ot all attacks on state education can be as easily dismissed as Ken Clarke's and Chris Woodhead's creative statistics or Melanie Phillip's eccentric approach to evidence. Serious questions have to be addressed about the use of the extra funding of schools in recent years, the performance of the most disadvantaged schools and the state of education in London. Also no defence of state schools would be complete without consideration of their performance *vis-à-vis* the independent sector.

Recent claims that extra money channelled into the system by government has been wasted is a damaging attack on state education. It ignores the significant underfunding of schools for so many years. Britain was the only one of twenty leading industrial countries where spending on education did not increase in real terms over a near twenty-year period from 1970 to 1988. In 2001, judged by the percentage of gross domestic product spent on schools, Britain was still fifteenth out of 26 countries (OECD, 2004 p199). Even by 2002 when increased finance was starting to filter through, our position had risen only to fourteenth out of 29, hardly evidence of the uncontrolled spending spree so often described. Britain still trailed Belgium, France, Switzerland and the USA, among others. Significantly, all four Scandinavian countries, seen as having amongst the most successful education systems in the world, were ahead of Britain in spending (OECD, 2005 p200).

Gross underspending on schools in the last quarter of the twentieth century meant that an enormous backlog of repairs and school building had accumulated. Thousands of children were using outside toilets whilst in some Bradford schools children were sitting under chicken wire to protect them from falling ceiling plaster.

The claim that extra spending has not produced improvement is untrue. In 2004 the OECD noted that the UK was a country with 'moderate expenditure on education per student' but had one of the highest levels of performance for pupils (OECD, 2004 p198). In 2000 Nick Davies, while attacking the continuing social divide in urban secondary schools, agreed that 'there is little doubt that in the last ten years there has been some real advance in standards in Britain's state schools' (Davies, 2000 p151).

The present government has concentrated spending on deprived urban areas through programmes such as Excellence in Cities. The approach has been crude, allocating some urban LEAs money for schools which serve wealthy suburbs. Even so, whilst enormous gaps persist between the performance of schools in the poorest and wealthiest areas, the fastest improvement has actually taken place in the poorer areas. Professor Stephen Gorard of York University has criticised the common belief that the gap between the highest and lowest achieving schools has grown (Gorard, 1997 pp7-13). He points out that when the *rate of improvement* (the proportionate change) is considered, rather than the raw numerical differences between groups of schools, a very different picture emerges. This runs counter to the arguments of Nick Davies, who looked at the social and educational divide in Sheffield and perceived a widening gap between the most and least successful schools. Although Davies was undoubtedly right to highlight the correlation between poverty and under-achievement in school, it is clear that his conclusions about a growing gulf between high-attaining, largely middle-class schools and lower attaining schools serving poorer children are unduly pessimistic.

GCSE results for three Yorkshire LEAs, Sheffield, Bradford and Hull for 2002 and 2005 are revealing. Two, Sheffield and Bradford, are relatively socially divided cities. Sheffield has a sharp east-west division with wealthy western suburbs, famously described by Betjeman as the most beautiful in England, reaching into the Peak District National Park. Bradford has a large ethnic minority population living largely in the inner city but there are extensive middle-class suburbs stretching beyond Ilkley into the Dales. Hull is socially very different from the other two. Its middle-class suburbs lie outside the city boundary and are mainly served by East Riding LEA comprehensive schools.

In Table 8, the average GCSE results (percentage of higher grade GCSEs) are summarised for the five highest and the five lowest attaining comprehensive schools in each city for 2002 and 2005, and the gap shown between the two years and the proportionate change this gap represented.

Table 8: Comparison of highest and lowest attaining schools in three Yorkshire cities: 2002 and 2005 (figures in percentages)

City	Highest attaining GCSE				Lowest attaining GCSE			
	02	05	gap	prop. change	02	05	gap	prop. change
Bradford	69.4	79	9.6	0.14	17.2	21.6	4.4	0.25
Hull	50.2	62.4	12.2	0.24	14.4	31.6	17.2	1.19
Sheffield	67.8	74.4	6.6	0.10	21.4	33.4	12.0	0.56

These figures support Stephen Gorard's view of the trend in the social and academic divide in English schools. The attainment gap between the two groups of schools, largely mirroring differences between the socio-economic circumstances of their pupil populations, is stark. Yet in all three authorities the rate of progress amongst the lower attaining schools, as indicated by the ratio between the 2002 and 2005 figures, is higher. In Hull and Sheffield, even the raw gap between the figures for the two years is wider for the lower attainers than for the higher. The survey suggests other reasons for optimism. All six sets of figures show significant improvement over a relatively short period. The improvement for low attaining schools in Hull is startling. Nor have international comparisons supported Davies' pessimistic view. Emma Smith has demonstrated that the attainment gap between the poorest pupils and the rest in this country is actually the third lowest of fourteen countries in western Europe (Smith, 2005 pp35-7).

Some of the most marked improvement has been in London. Teachers know that the national political and media agenda on education is driven largely by the situation in London. Journalists and columnists with the national press, who mainly live in London, appear to know little and care less about thousands of schools outside the capital, except when the occasional tragedy strikes. The wholly disproportionate emphasis placed on parental choice arises largely from ministers' experiences in London and has little relevance to the needs of parents in huge swathes of rural Northumberland, Devon, Cumbria or North Yorkshire.

Many people outside London fail to appreciate the challenges facing its schools or the progress made in recent years. London includes some of the poorest local authorities in the country alongside the richest: the percentage of children eligible for free school meals across inner London is three times the national average. The proportion of children who speak English as an additional language, remarked by HMI in the 50s when it was 3 per cent in one school, is now 50 per cent in inner London and 30 per cent in outer London. Children in the capital speak over three hundred different languages.

One in seven London children attend independent schools, twice the national average, but in some areas the figure is closer to one in three, turning many comprehensive schools into virtual secondary moderns and creating huge gaps between the highest and lowest performing schools. Teacher recruitment and retention is an enormous problem for London schools.

In spite of these huge obstacles, London schools are amongst the fastest improving in the country: schools in two boroughs, Lewisham and Islington, are the most improved in the country. Professor Tim Brighouse, Chief Adviser to London Challenge, which co-ordinates school improvement across London, points out that since 1979 the increase in the percentage of children getting five higher grade GCSEs in inner London has been nearly double that of Oxfordshire.

Lilian Baylis Technology College in Lambeth, for instance, has faced formidable challenges over recent years. Three quarters of its children are on free school meals and 95 per cent from ethnic minorities, a quarter of whom are refugees or asylum seekers. The school had six head teachers in five years up to 2001 (*TES*, 02/06/06). Yet under the leadership of the present head, Gary Philips, it has raised the percentage of children achieving higher grade GCSEs from six to thirty six in four years. Its pupils are making outstanding progress. The school offers a tremendous programme of extra-curricular activities and has made great strides in improving behaviour.

Peter Hyman left a prestigious post as one of the inner circle of Tony Blair's advisers in Downing Street to work as a teaching assistant at another inner London school, Islington Green (Hyman, 2005). This school too has a skewed intake, the implications of which make a mockery of shallow attacks in the national press on so called 'comprehensive schools'. The majority of pupils are in the bottom third of the ability range and 95 per cent are working class. Half are on free meals, despite the school being close to some of the most expensive private housing in Europe. Forty languages are spoken and over a third of the children speak English as an additional language. Hyman, who had seen ministers dealing with the most intractable of problems at first hand, immediately recognised the leadership qualities of the head, Trevor Averre-Beeson; the number and demanding nature of the different roles played and the 'hundred decisions a day' to be taken. Hyman was equally impressed by the classroom performance of teachers:

> At a school like this, with a lot of difficult children, the sheer will power from teachers is extra-ordinary... Some are stricter, some more inter-active, but all have a presence and a command. Their lessons have a pace that carries you along with them. (Hyman, 2005 p118)

Despite the challenges posed by London schools, research by the National Foundation for Educational Research found that 80 per cent of children and 90 per cent of teachers enjoyed working and studying in London schools (Ridley, 2005). Teachers in London were also twice as likely to say that the quality of their school had improved in the past year than to say it had declined.

Some of the strongest attacks on state schools compare their academic performance to that of independent schools. Chris Woodhead notes that fee-paying schools regularly occupy the top twenty positions in the GCSE performance tables and achieve over four times the proportion of A* and A grades of state schools (Woodhead, 2002 p29). Their domination of the A-level tables is even greater, with 47 of the top 50 places taken by schools from the independent sector. Even the introduction of value-added performance tables, showing the progress pupils make as opposed to raw examination scores, has not dented the apparent superiority of the private sector.

Most of the relative success of independent schools can be explained by academic selection. True, a handful of schools outside the mainstream of independents choose deliberately to be academically, if not socially, comprehensive and some of those at the bottom end of the market have no choice to be otherwise if they are to survive. Nevertheless, the schools which dominate the league tables are in effect independent grammar schools and highly selective ones at that. The head of one of the most academically successful independent schools has said that nearly all of his pupils came from the top 2 per cent of the ability range – the equivalent of the top fifth of a typical state grammar school. Nick Davies quotes the head of Roedean, which is often seen as a more socially than academically exclusive school, as saying that all her pupils were above average academically, 'many significantly so' (Davies, 2000 p70).

Parents of children at independent schools, over 90 per cent of whom pay full fees, largely come from affluent professional backgrounds and are highly educated themselves; key factors in any child's educational success. Stephen Gorard found that in Wales nearly half of all mothers and nearly two thirds of fathers of independent school pupils had university degrees, which is well above the Welsh average (Gorard, 1997 p218). Contrast that with the position described in the early 1980s by the head of a school in a deprived part of north Manchester who said that the parents of his fifth year, of nearly 200 pupils, possessed not a single O-level amongst them!

Nevertheless, recent research by Professor David Jessen of York University does pose a challenge to the state sector. In 2005 he looked at the performance of the brightest 5 per cent of 11 year-olds at KS2, and later at GCSE and A-level. He found that virtually all the independently educated children amongst them went on to achieve five or more A* or A grades at GCSE and three As at A-level, whereas only two thirds of state school pupils reached the same standard at GCSE and fewer than a third at A-level. Predictably, the news led to headlines telling of 'comprehensive failure' and 'brightest failed by state schools' (*TES*, 02/12/05).

But the implications of Jessen's findings may not be as clearcut as appears. Professor Tymms points out that the top 5 per cent of the entire child population contains a wide spread of ability from the highly gifted to the intelligent hardworking. There is evidence to suggest that a disproportionate number of the most highly able (the top 1 or 2 per cent, as suggested above) may attend independent schools. Even fifty years ago the Crowther committee found independent schools had far more of the brightest 10 per cent of children than state grammar schools (Crowther, 1959 p199). State schools are also under greater pressure to succeed in national curriculum tests and may have pushed borderline children into higher levels in the KS2 tests, more than private schools which are under no obligation even to enter pupils. Professor Geoff Whitty, who researched comparative A-level performance at independent and state schools, found a difference of just over half a grade per subject in favour of the former. He comments

> What is remarkable is how *small* the difference is when you consider factors that distinguish state comprehensive schools from the ...elite private schools in our study...the nature of intakes, class sizes, qualifications of teachers, their facilities etc.

> ...if the most able children in comprehensive schools can perform neck and neck with.. and in some case outperform..those in schools with a mission directly geared to their needs, how ...is it that comprehensive schools are presented as failing? (Whitty, 2006 p58)

Nor could Whitty's or Jesson's research cover a key element in the success of any child: the degree of parental motivation and support. Some years ago, I asked a parent to come and see me whose 14 year-old son, 'Fred Brown', was causing us concern. To our surprise, because we had previously experienced great difficulty in persuading him to come to school, Mr Brown agreed to meet me. Straightaway he told me that Fred would not trouble us further: he would be departing school and education forever. Despite all my arguments, including the illegality of his action, Mr Brown was adamant. He believed that all education after the age of 12 was a total waste of time. Soon after, Fred disappeared and despite the best efforts of my staff and educational social workers, who asked that he be kept on the register so that he would not disappear from the system, was never seen in any school again.

All comprehensive headteachers, however favoured their catchment areas, will have met Mr Browns. The head of one successful school said that a pupil's father had told him that when he was at school he had truanted for fifteen months and saw no harm in it. Another colleague told of how two families in his school had recently taken their year 11 children away on holiday, not simply during mock examinations, but for the entire GCSE examination period in June. In some authorities with large ethnic minorities it has been common practice for children to return for extended visits, sometimes for months, to their country of origin.

Mr Brown was not typical and who knows what negative experiences during his own time at school had influenced him? The real victim was Fred. However, the story throws light on how schools are compared. Fred Brown's disappearance lost the school a percentage point in the performance tables. Had value-added systems figures, showing pupil progress, been published at the time his absence would have had an even more negative effect because he achieved levels at KS2 and KS3 but not at GCSE (KS4).

Independent schools struggle with parents who expect to hand over the entire responsibility for their child's education to the school, whilst others have ludicrously inflated expectations of their offspring's likely results simply because they are paying fees. What independent and grammar schools do not face, however, is the challenge of parents like Mr Brown who regard the entire process of education as irrelevant. Chris Woodhead and other commentators fail to appreciate that it only takes a handful of Freds in a comprehensive school to reduce its examination performance to a point where however successful it is with other pupils, it will never match the highest performing independent and grammar schools.

All international evidence points to three factors which strongly influence whether a child succeeds academically at school. They are

- the child's academic attainment on entry to the school
- family income and social class
- parental educational achievement

Yet how many independent schools have significant numbers of children who fall into the lowest twenty-five per cent of the population in all three categories? And how many comprehensive schools have no such children? Most people would agree that the answer to the first question is virtually none. There might be less consensus, over the second question. References are frequently made to some comprehensives being 'middle-class' or situated in 'leafy suburbs'. The implication is that they teach only academic, middle class children. Yet this applies to only a handful of schools across the country. There are very few comprehensive schools which do not take significant numbers of pupils from that lowest quartile. There are schools with GCSE results over 80 per cent, where many pupils are accepted each year at the most selective universities, which also have surprising numbers of pupils from socially and academically disadvantaged families with major educational special needs. These pupils would neither apply to, nor be accepted by, most independent schools.

The apparent superiority of independent schools and grammar schools in valued-added measures is even easier to explain. Selective schools, which include most independents, will understandably question whether a pupil making very poor progress is in the right institution and may even ask parents to remove them. Comprehensive schools cannot legally exclude a child for academic reasons nor should they. The emphasis is placed by most of them on inclusion. Such numbers do not need to be large to influence school performance. One or two bright pupils seriously under-performing can make a significant negative impact to the value-added figures for an entire year group.

A school full of high-achieving pupils will always succeed in tables based on progress as well as in those measuring only raw attainment. Bright children progress on average at a faster rate, as well as starting from a higher point, as the Cockcroft report noted years ago (Cockcroft, 1982 pp99-100). It is more likely, regardless of the school attended, that a child who has reached level 4 in tests at 11 will progress to level 6 by 14, than that a child on level 3 at the same age will reach level 5 three years later.

Attitudes to inclusion also explain much of the difference between the sectors at A-level. As well as selecting on entry to the school, most independent schools select again at 16. The intake of comprehensive schools sixth forms is normally far wider, including students who would not have been accepted at most independent schools at 11 or 13 let alone into the sixth form. Many independent sixth forms are small. A quarter of the *Financial Times* list of the top 500 selective schools in 2005 had fewer than thirty students entered for A-level.

The size of the independent sector is often exaggerated by the media, possibly because fee-paying schools are based disproportionately in the south-east and London, where most commentators live. Whilst relatively small increases in the number of children at fee-paying schools are widely publicised, the total of 7 per cent of school age children attending private schools has remained largely unchanged in fifty years. It is barely higher than the average figure for all OECD countries at 6 per cent. Independent education *is* expensive in Britain. Nevertheless, the small size of the sector and its relatively static size over time is hardly a convincing argument for the supposed decline in state education, particularly given the huge rise in real disposable incomes in recent decades. Ironically the largest boost to independent school numbers came, not as a result of comprehensive education in the 1960s or later, but in the 1940s and early 50s as middle-class parents fled the threat of secondary moderns.

Biased press reporting of the two sectors was never more evident than over the accusation that certain universities were discriminating against applications from independent school students. One *Daily Mail* headline on the issue read 'The March of the Social Engineers' (01/10/02) whilst a later editorial claimed 'the regrettable truth is that too many state schools cannot teach to the necessary standard' (03/10/04). This ignored several other inconvenient 'truths'. On average, state school applicants to the most competitive universities have A-level results which are just as good as successful independent school candidates, while thousands of others who fail to get in to these universities have as good results as those who do. The *Mail* (in 2004) also ignored research at Warwick University in 2002, which found that state school students achieve on average better degree results than those from the independent sector with the same A-level grades (Naylor and Smith, 2002).

Sensibly, the Independent Schools Council launched a full investigation into the whole affair, looking at 300 university courses, involving 20,000 applicants. They found the charges to be completely unfounded. A representative stated: 'The figures show no evidence of discrimination against independent school candidates either in the percentage of candidates offered places or in the grade required' (*The Guardian*, 17/08/05).

Unusually, several papers which normally feature statements from independent sector representatives prominently, found little or no space for this report when it was published. Few people today appreciate that as late as the

60s many Oxbridge colleges openly stated that they would always give pre-ference to applicants who had 'family connections' with the college. The phrase, 'social engineering' was never mentioned in this context.

Many of those who criticise state schools today point to a return to selection as the way forward. But new research from David Jesson has shown that the remaining fifteen or so local authorities, predominantly in wealthy areas, which have retained selective schools today are actually under-performing compared with fully comprehensive systems. He notes that

> ...pupils in selective areas, with a few ...exceptions, achieve much lower examination results than similar pupils educated in genuinely comprehen-sive schools. When this finding is linked with earlier work showing that the ablest pupils in comprehensive schools do as well, if not better than similar pupils in grammar schools, it is clear there is a very real issue of under-performance in these schools. (Jesson, 2006 p117)

Professor Jesson also points out that the perceived performance of the com-prehensive sector has been affected by the designation of some schools in selective areas as comprehensive when they are really secondary moderns (p111).

The argument over how well our schools are doing need not be confined to the classroom. In Britain, as in the rest of the world, there is agreement that education matters – crucially so. Whilst the issue may not always top most voters' priorities, it normally features in the top three or four. Most heads are used to themselves and their schools being blamed for many national ills, be it crime and anti-social behaviour or lack of competitiveness in the economy or sport. But this criticism is not new. In one form or another it has now been levelled at the education system for over forty years. This raises an intriguing question.

If it is true that ideologues in teaching, opposed to excellence, competition or real learning have, alongside hordes of incompetents, wrought havoc across the nation's classrooms since the mid-60s, then they would have wrecked the education of practically everyone under the age of 50. In this case wouldn't the results be far more evident in the state of British society today?

Some critics are only too eager to produce evidence of just such an outcome. A significant section of the population seems to exist in what one political adviser called 'a near permanent state of self-righteous anger'. Spleen is vented over issues as diverse as binge drinking and increases in violent crime, 'dumbing down' in the arts and media, the state of public transport, defeats on the sports field and on and on. Newspaper columnists, editorials, readers' letters, and comments on phone-ins complain continually about almost every aspect of national life. One of the most popular Christmas books in 2005 was elegantly titled *Is it just me or is everything just shite?* Millions watch TV programmes entitled *Grumpy Old Men* or *Women*. Schools are not the only, or even the major target, of complaints. Usually it is the current government, of whichever party, but education is certainly one favourite butt of the critics.

This downbeat view of the state of the country today mirrors the distorted view of state schools. There is a wealth of positive evidence about Britain today, of which only a few examples can be offered here. The economy is the fourth largest in the world after the USA, Japan and Germany, although China is rapidly catching up with all four. Our GDP per capita, a more accurate guide to real national wealth, whilst trailing that of wealthy countries with small populations like Switzerland, Norway and Austria, is third only to the USA and Japan amongst the largest nations and much higher than the average for the euro-zone. Inflation has averaged 4 per cent over the past twenty-five years, less than half that of the previous period.

Britain remains a relatively racially tolerant country, although we should not be complacent. Tony Barnes, head of Park High, an ethnically mixed school in Harrow, said he believes race relations in north west London to be as good overall as anywhere, a view perhaps shared by the International Olympic Committee in awarding the 2012 games to London. It would be inconceivable for the crude racist abuse which is common in some continental football stadia not to be addressed in this country.

Large provincial cities have been completely transformed in the past two decades, with Newcastle, Manchester, Birmingham, Leeds and Sheffield improving beyond recognition. Britain remains one of the foremost artistic and cultural centres of the world, whether in music, both classical and popular, drama, art or literature. The sheer number of works in translation by British authors in overseas bookshops is staggering. Our so-called sporting decline compared with the post-war years is a myth, as shown in chapter 10.

Above all, those outside this country do not subscribe to the negative view of Britain. The Anholt survey for GMI in February 2006, 'How the world sees the world' sought views on a huge range of human activities and attributes including, significantly, education. Over 25,000 people across the world were asked to rank other countries according to how positively they regarded them under different headings. The UK was placed first amongst 35 countries, ahead of Switzerland and Canada, and was also ranked in the top five in the survey in most other countries. No other country approached such a consistently favourable level of response. Nor was this particular survey a one-off: previous studies by the same group had always placed Britain in the top four. A later survey in 2006, which included only EU countries, again placed the UK first (www.nationbrandindex.com).

No doubt some would claim that not only are these positive elements countered by the many failings of national life but that they exist despite, rather than because of, our educational system. This suggests some consistency might reasonably be demanded of these critics. If state schools are not to receive credit for the under-reported and frequently unappreciated positive features of life in modern Britain, nor should they bear the burden of responsibility for its negative aspects .

8
Bottom of the class?

When examining the performance of state schools in England an important area for consideration must be how they measure up to those abroad. Yet comparisons of educational performance across frontiers are fraught with pitfalls. Historical, cultural, demographic, social and economic differences all lead to varying interpretations of even apparently straightforward terminology, let alone of more complex issues like teaching methods, curriculum and assessment. For example, the belief that maths is culturally neutral and therefore a suitable vehicle for international comparative testing has been shown by Professor Margaret Brown of Kings College, London, to be a myth (Brown, 1998 p43). These difficulties have not stopped critics of state schools using international assessment as a weapon against our schools, or attacking the methodology of the tests when they have emerged favourably in them.

This chapter examines the findings of recent international comparative studies of school and pupil performance, the experience of visits to schools abroad and from those by foreign teachers to this country. Some wider lessons for school improvement from this evidence are drawn.

In the past decade there have been at least six major international assessment programmes, involving the testing of hundreds of thousands of pupils across dozens of countries. Whilst the picture presented by these studies of the performance of children in this country is mixed, important positive features have emerged. Our performance, in relation to those countries with which direct comparisons with England can reasonably be made, is surprisingly good. Additionally, standards relative to other countries appear to be improving rather than deteriorating. Many of the countries taking part in the international testing, which has grown so popular since the 1990s, cannot reasonably be compared with this country. Levels of deprivation in South Africa, Mexico or Belize are obviously such that the weaker performance of their pupils in tests can tell us little about our own schools. Equally, the test results of a country such as Liechtenstein, with the population of a small English market town, throw no light on how English schools are faring.

The leading positions in the test are often taken by the successful economies of the Pacific Rim, Scandinavian countries or other European states with low levels of deprivation such as Austria or Switzerland. Many of the most successful educational systems are in states such as Finland, which is less populated than London and which lacks the sprawling conurbations, extremes of poverty and high crime levels of countries like Britain, France or the USA. Cultural and historical differences, well beyond the power of schools to influence, also affect performance. Observers of one international test in South Korea reported pupils marching into the examination hall to the strains of the school band, past rows of national flags, after a stirring speech from their headteacher. Meanwhile, across the Pacific, American students complained long and loudly about the loss of a popular games session which was replaced by the test (Brown, 1998 p44).

To get closer to the truth of how England actually performs in international terms, our performance in tests was compared with a group of countries with which this country has most in common, culturally, economically, socially and politically. These were the seven other G8 nations, Canada, France, Germany, the USA, Japan, Italy and Russia and additionally, three other leading English-speaking nations with which this country has close cultural and historical ties, Australia, Ireland and New Zealand. Finally the Netherlands was added. Whilst neither a member of the G8 nor English speaking (at least not as a first language), it is a wealthy neighbour with high-performing schools, has close ties to Britain and faces similar social challenges. The population, twenty million, though smaller than the UK, France or Germany, is much closer to ours than Switzerland, Singapore or Finland. This group of countries can tell us more about our real international standing than lengthy tables, including countries as economically, culturally and geographically diverse from the UK and each other as Chile, Estonia or Thailand.

The relative performance of the twelve countries, including England, was examined in nineteen separate tests taken between 1995 and 2003. The tests were taken as part of six studies organised by the Organisation for Economic and Cultural Development (OECD), a UN agency and the International Association for the Evaluation of Educational Achievement (IEA), based in Boston, Massachusetts.

In 1995 and 2003, the IEA organised the Trends in International Maths and Science Survey (TIMSS), testing 10 and 14 year-olds in maths and science, and in 1999 14 year-olds alone. It also organised the Progress in International Reading Literacy Survey (PIRLS) in 2001 for older primary children. The OECD ran the Programme of International Student Achievement (PISA), testing literacy, maths and science for 15 year-olds in 2000 and again in 2003 with an emphasis on maths. Several of the surveys involved extensive questionnaires for schools, pupils and parents, which provide a valuable source of data from across the world on what helps or hinders pupil performance.

Table 9 shows the average ranking of the eleven comparison countries plus England against all countries participating in the tests (column A) and their relative standing against each other (column B)

Table 9: Performances in international school tests: 1995-2003

Comparison Group	Total tests taken	Column A	Column B
AUSTRALIA	18	10.1	3
CANADA	19	11.7	5
FRANCE	9	17.7	10
GERMANY	9	18.7	11
IRELAND	12	13.4	6
ITALY	9	21.5	12
JAPAN	18	3.7	1
NETHERLANDS	16	6.4	2
NEW ZEALAND	18	15.5	8
RUSSIA	14	17.5	9
USA	19	14	7
ENGLAND	19	11.5	4

Column A: Average rank order amongst all countries participating

Column B: Average rank order amongst comparison group only

Average number of countries participating in tests 32

A comparative exercise like this must be treated with caution. France, Germany and Italy all took part in fewer tests than the other countries. But the nine tests which were taken in these countries covered all three strands, literacy, maths and science, as well as age groups ranging from ages 10 to 15. Furthermore, the results have caused much soul searching in all three countries: their relatively weak performances have not been dismissed as a statistical aberration. The results of the 2003 PISA tests for England were included, even though the number of schools taking part were too small for our results to be officially included. (The figures did not improve our overall standing.)

It is clear that the performance of English pupils in the tests across the last decades has been more impressive than is often recognised. Where credit has been given, it has been grudging. Whilst it has been accepted that our pupils are performing in the top third of *all* participating countries, attention has been drawn to the presence of participants such as Tunisia or Serbia. The implication persists that the satisfactory standing of schools in England, when faced with such competition, is hardly a cause of pride. But what Table 9 suggests is that English pupils out-perform, or at least match those of the richest, most successful countries in the world.

At the time of writing, the results also offer tentative hope that our relative position may be improving. Whilst our average position among all the countries taking part in the ten tests between 1995 and 1999 was 14.4, in the nine taken in the early years of this century it has risen to 8.4. Whilst it is clear that results from our schools in literacy are always better than those in maths, regardless of the age of the pupils, the evidence points to a strong performance by English children.

Few attempts have been made to assess the performance of pupils across all tests in this way. More commonly, each new set of tests has led to fresh arguments about their validity and what they reveal about the state of English education. The greatest controversy was created by the PISA tests in literacy, maths and science in 2000. English 15 year-olds came seventh in literacy, eighth in maths and fourth in science. Doubts about the methodology and assessment methods were raised by Professor Sig Prais (Prais, 2003). The performance of schools in England was well above average for this particular group of tests which did seem to favour native English speakers. Australia, Canada, Ireland and New Zealand all recorded their best results in the PISA 2000 tests, although not the USA. But Prais questioned these tests in other ways. He queried the validity of the English sample. Low participation rates by English schools have proved a problem for the organisers of international testing. Despite suspicions that this is the result of government sabotage of the process to cover up low standards, the decision to participate is taken at school level, unlike those countries with more centralised educational systems. The reluctance of heads to take part is due to the tests taking place in early summer, when English secondary schools struggle under the weight of external examinations.

Professor Prais stated that the need to replace so many schools in the original sample suggested that 'The missing schools, on the whole were probably low attainers... there must be grave suspicions of upward bias in the average score of responding schools' (p149).

So was the English sample simply more able than those of other countries and the results artificially inflated? No evidence was produced for this claim, repeated by think tanks like Civitas and Reform and several newspaper columnists. None appeared to have read the actual PISA report. Had they done so they would have learnt that the assumption made by Professor Prais was wrong. The response rate was actually lower amongst higher attaining schools (see Adams, 2003).

Table 10: School response rate in PISA 2000 (England)

State schools

With fewer than 42 per cent of students with 5 or more GCSEs at A*-C:	62 per cent
With more than 43 per cent of students with 5 or more GCSEs at A*-C:	50 per cent
All independent schools:	51 per cent

(Gill *et al*, 2002 p150)

Comparison of the number of children on free school meals in schools initially approached by the organisers of PISA reveal that schools which agreed to participate had more poor children than those which declined. Although its sampling was not criticised by Professor Prais, the PIRLS tests of 10 year-olds in 2001 also had a similar response pattern to PISA 2000, with lower attaining schools and those with more children from poor families more likely to take part than others. The assumption that within schools less able children would have been more reluctant to take the test does not fit at all with my own experience. Our school was selected as part of the sample for PISA 2003. We did participate and ensured that practically all those selected took the tests. But it was difficult to persuade the brightest pupils, especially in Year 11, some taking ten GCSEs, to sit yet another test in the run-up to public examinations.

The suggestion by Prais that the PISA organisers were wrong to organise their testing on the basis of age groups rather than year groups, as most previous surveys including the TIMSS series had done, is even less convincing. He argues that this approach penalises those countries 'which group pupils into classes having regard to their maturation' (Prais, 2003 p146): in other words, which make the weakest students repeat a school year. But what Prais ignores is that assessing pupils by year group places countries like England, where students do not normally repeat years, at an enormous disadvantage. Margaret Brown has pointed out that this led to a staggering 20 per cent of the weakest pupils being excluded from nine out of 39 countries, including France and Germany, in the TIMSS tests in 1995. The corresponding figure for England was 1 per cent (Brown, 1998 p40). The effect of this on the results is immense.

Prais also points out that the choice of a single age for testing, 15, may invalidate results in countries like Switzerland and Germany where some 15 year-olds would be in part-time employment and impossible to access. But is he suggesting that, had they been included, these early leavers would have actually raised the average performance of students from these countries? It seems unlikely.

In summary, whilst the findings of PISA 2000 have been challenged, the basis for the attack seems weak. And even if the results of PISA 2000 are omitted from the analysis in Table 6, England's average position in the rank order of all countries only drops to 13.1 and by one place, to fifth, amongst the comparison group.

PISA also revealed a great deal about why some students do so much better than others at school (OECD, 2001). Whilst many of the findings seem common sense and have been generally accepted within Britain for decades, it is helpful to see these conclusions confirmed by data collected on a global scale. In addition, not all the PISA answers to why pupils succeed or fail are as obvious as others.

That parental occupation and wealth was the major determinant of a pupil's success at school was hardly a surprise. Less welcome news in England was that, despite our overall good showing in the tests, the effect was greater than in all but five of the 31 countries taking part. The level of education of parents, particularly the mother and especially when she had been educated to the equivalent of A-level , was another key indicator of a child's likely success. Alongside education, the existence of cultural items in the home such as books and works of art as well as the extent of communication between parents and children about cultural issues and current and social affairs also influence a child's success. In many families more than one of these characteristics co-exist. Other negative aspects of students' backgrounds present a massive challenge for schools and policy makers. For example, PISA found that whilst living with one parent is usually associated with lower performance in school everywhere, the effect is far greater in the UK and USA than elsewhere.

Conversely, the negative educational effect of being born outside the country of residence or of having parents who were born outside the country is less in the UK than elsewhere. Our schools are shown to compensate well for the effects on children of having parents who are poorly educated or have emigrated here but are less effective in dealing with the negative impact of growing up in a one parent family or one which is poor.

PISA also considered which type of school organisation is more effective. Whilst the conclusions are tentative, they suggest that the overall effect of selecting children for schools according to their ability is to depress results. The countries which had the greatest variation in performance between schools were Belgium, Germany, Hungary and Austria, where selecting children for different schools by ability is common. The least variation appeared in Iceland, Sweden, Finland and Norway, which do not select. But there was also a clear positive link between non-selection and high achievement. Whilst not proving that comprehensive systems are superior to selective ones, this should certainly give pause for thought to those who so confidently argue the opposite case.

What is clear from evidence from PISA and from other studies is that non-institutional features, especially family background, are by far the largest determinants of children's performance at school. It seems, across the world, factors outside the school gates determine around three quarters of how well a child does. In addition, as Richard Hatcher notes, the distinctions between factors the school apparently can and cannot control are far from clear cut (cited in Wrigley, 2003 p16). Reactions to these findings will differ. Some will even see it as proof that schools hardly matter. And yet the influence of educators, even if less than sometimes thought, is still enormous. Apart from the 25 per cent of academic achievement schools do determine, the effect of the school on areas which are of far more importance than any tests, the moral, spiritual and cultural development of the child, is impossible to calculate.

My interest in education abroad stems from the 1960s when I took up my first teaching post in an international school in Switzerland. A less naïve candidate might have queried the speed with which my application was met with the reply that I was the 'ideal person for the post', even though I was neither interviewed nor had my references taken up. The school's mission statement – had such things existed then – would have been admirable in its simplicity if nothing else: to make as much money for the proprietors as possible. One student's father received an invoice which included 'use of television: 240 Swiss francs'. There were fifty girls in her house, each being charged £20 to watch TV. One old black and white set was generating £1000 a year – in 1966!

Working at the school taught me a great deal about getting on with people of different nationalities but little about standards in schools abroad.

Years later, as head of a comprehensive school, I visited schools in Austria and the Czech Republic and university departments of education in France, and met dozens of teachers, especially from Germany and Scandinavia, who regularly visited schools in York. I taught, and talked to many students from overseas who joined my school's sixth form and discussed with other heads and teachers their own experiences of educational visits to other countries. In all these encounters I sought views on school values, academic standards, teaching methods, student behaviour and school organisation. It would be unrealistic to accept at face value the comments of overseas visitors to a school. Most were, of course, polite and highly complimentary. I found that asking for ideas for improvement, rather than for direct criticisms opened up discussion and revealed their real opinions of our schools. In all these meetings and visits I found little evidence that the overall standards and breadth of education in the countries in question were thought to be higher than those in the English state system.

I also witnessed examples of weaknesses, often thought to be peculiarly English, such as wide variations in the standards of teaching. Together with several other heads and inspectors from countries across Europe I visited a school in Austria. The local education director told us that it was the most academically successful school, state or independent, in a province which had a population of three-quarters of a million, more than most English counties. We saw excellent teaching. One superb biology lesson was taught in English to a class of enthusiastic Year 7 pupils. But there were also lessons which, though selected for us beforehand by the school, were as bad as anything I have ever witnessed in a English classroom. One group of youngsters in an ICT lesson were browsing the internet to no purpose, drifting through sites on pop music or football, with no direction or help from the teacher. I assumed, wrongly, that he must have been covering for an absent colleague, rather than an ICT specialist teaching his own class.

Another lesson was simply embarrassing. The head took four of us into a science laboratory. A young teacher had completely lost control of a class despite the presence of the head of department at the back of the room, obviously there to keep order. Eventually there were six adults in the room, including three headteachers. We were completely ignored by twenty or so of the brightest youngsters in eastern Austria, who shouted across the lab, laughed loudly and cheered ironically the attempts by the unfortunate young teacher to regain control. We were led out after a short time without comment.

I have no feeling of *schadenfreude* in recounting these incidents. Poor and undisciplined lessons have taken place in all the schools I have taught in and led, including some I have taught. What I reject is the trite assumption in the media that at other times and in other countries these problems have been resolved and that only incompetence or misguided ideology prevents a similar outcome here. Later, the visiting group from as far afield as Spain, Bulgaria, Finland and Italy all agreed the variation in teaching ability and pupil behaviour we had just witnessed was wholly typical of schools at home.

Students who joined my own school's sixth form, many from Germany, France, Italy and Scandinavia, often expressed the view, unprompted, that they preferred teaching approaches in England. They welcomed the greater opportunities for class discussion, despite all the constraints of modular A-levels. Interestingly, it was often the brightest students who most welcomed the move away from what they saw as the over-didactic and formal approach of teachers at home. Many, despite initially coming for one year, wanted to stay into the Upper Sixth.

I was also shocked by some of the outdated social attitudes I came across. In a vocational gymnasium (grammar school) in a small Austrian town I met a group of bright 18 year old girls in a business studies class. I asked them what they intended to do after school. It seemed that none were considering university. I pointed out that in my own school, it would be assumed students like themselves would at least be thinking about the possibility of higher education. When I raised the issue later with the principal, he seemed un-concerned. He shrugged and said, 'Well they are all very attractive; no doubt their parents will be thinking they will be married before long'.

Later, the rest of our group was divided over this incident. A Finnish inspector was appalled and the director of education for the area, who was hosting the visit, thought what had been said was not untypical and was a major concern for him. Others were indifferent and none seemed really shocked. Admittedly this was only one incident, but it did not indicate high expectations of half the student population.

In dealings with overseas teachers, including many who had taught in Britain, I met none who believed that state schools and teachers here were generally poor. There were certainly many who shared my view that our children are ludicrously over-tested. Others, whilst accepting the need for inspection and schools to be accountable, thought there was an unjustified and unpleasant culture of mistrusting teachers here. A recent best-seller in Germany is en-titled *The teacher hater book* so we may no longer be alone in this! At the same time I heard frequent references from colleagues from other countries to the vitality of classrooms here, the excellent relations between teachers and pupils, the richness of extra-curricular opportunities and, yes, the high academic standards they encountered.

This is why there is so much interest in visiting and working in schools in this country. The Czech Republic publishes figures for requests from Czech teachers to visit other European countries on European Union sponsored study visits. Applications to visit Britain were boosted by opportunities to improve English language skills. Equally, the dominance of Russian over many years means that Czech teachers now need to improve their German, the language of their neighbours. Yet the number of requests to visit Britain outnumbered any other country and represented a quarter of the total and over twice the next largest. Czech officials were adamant that this resulted from the level of interest in the British schools.

A poll conducted by Harris in 2006 of several thousand people in the UK, Germany and Spain revealed much higher levels of satisfaction with state schools amongst parents in the UK than in the other two countries (BBC news website 07/03/06).

The figures showed 64 per cent as satisfied in the UK, compared with 44 per cent in Spain and 36 per cent in Germany. As with polls taken in this country, adults without children at state schools have lower levels of satisfaction: 42 per cent in the UK, 31 per cent in Spain and 22 per cent in Germany. This group, as the BBC's Mike Baker pointed out, do not see the reality of school life 'every day of the week (and) base their views on second hand information'. Even so, it is fascinating that people *without* children at state schools in this country actually have more favourable views than German parents who do have children at state schools.

None of this implies that we can't learn from schools and educational systems abroad. Arguments in favour of a more widely based diploma instead of our narrow A-level system, as recommended in the Tomlinson report, are overwhelming. Hong Kong, with one of the most effective education systems in the world, is now abandoning English GCSE and A-level in favour of a single diploma. Surely the narrow A-level diet which allows students to study, for instance, only English language, literature and media studies, cannot continue here. Vocational education, despite recent reforms here, is also more successful in many countries. Our foreign language skills remain amongst the worst in Europe. And it is significant that the state school system in Finland which is widely accepted as the most successful in the western world is so different from the educational vision promoted by much of our media and many politicians. It is fully comprehensive, characterised by high spending and low class sizes, lessons are relatively informal and there is no national inspectorate or league tables.

9

A whiteboard jungle

So far we have looked mainly at the academic performance of children in state schools. Yet for all the emphasis today on league tables and examination success, the sole aim of schools can never be to raise academic achievement, crucial as that is. An unknown Holocaust survivor famously captured the horror of learning which lacked moral foundations when he wrote of seeing 'gas chambers built by learned engineers... infants killed by trained nurses' and reflected

> I am suspicious of education.
> My request is: help your students become more human.
> Your efforts must never produce learned monsters..
> Reading, writing and arithmetic are important only
> If they serve to make our children more human.
> (quoted in Supple, 1993 p291)

Few would quarrel with these sentiments. If education is not about making young people more compassionate, more tolerant and better able to collaborate with others, it is nothing. If schools don't ensure that moral growth accompanies academic development at every stage, they have failed.

Yet the practical application of a moral vision, whether in faith schools like my own or community schools where the imperative to ensure that all children experience love, justice and hope is also recognised, can be daunting. To take an example which is all too familiar to every head: when does a school decide that the desperate needs of a child from an abusive, loveless home, who is aggressive and disruptive, are outweighed by the right of other pupils and staff not to suffer the consequences of her or his continued presence? Some of the most serious criticisms of state education suggest that we have got the balance wrong between compassion towards such damaged children and the right of the majority to be safe and have their education undisturbed. Many go further, suggesting that we are producing 'unlearned monsters'.

Certainly, there is a formidable body of evidence to suggest that the behaviour and moral attitudes of the young have deteriorated both inside and outside school. Surveys of secondary teachers reveal that almost all have had experience of dealing with disruptive pupils, and that many suffer stress or mental health problems afterwards (BBC news website 13/04/2006). The worst incidents have shocked the entire nation. Recent years have seen the most appalling criminal acts in or near schools, including the murders of a headteacher at his school gates and of a pupil in a quiet country school, several fatal stabbings near schools and the rape of a teacher by a pupil. In 2004 the annual report of the chief inspector of schools stated that the number of schools where behaviour was unsatisfactory had increased. This led to headlines such as 'Collapse of the classrooms as hooligans win power struggle' and 'Discipline in schools is worst ever'. These fears are confirmed by TV footage filmed by undercover reporters, equipped with hidden cameras, posing as supply teachers. Pupils have been shown out of control, disrupting classes and swearing at teachers and classmates.

Parents and children are acutely concerned about bullying. The Children's Commissioner for England told the BBC that, 'children put bullying top of the list of things they want me to be aware of.... they want bullying stopped now' (BBC news website 14/11/05).

Evidence that behaviour is worse in English schools than in the past is stronger than it is about deterioration in academic standards. Correspondents who contacted me via *Saga magazine* about their education after the war, a significant number of whom had serious reservations about aspects of their schooling, were generally agreed that discipline and behaviour were better when they were at school. Stan Noble recalled 'no examples of extreme pupil behaviour and classes were orderly'. Marian Margan said 'teachers demanded and mostly got silence in the classroom and refused to tolerate insubordination', whilst Margaret Clough was 'never in a class that had a discipline problem'. Even the Harris survey, quoted in chapter 8, showing British parents to be happier with state schools than parents in Germany or Spain, found the one exception was discipline, which they thought to be worse than the parents in other countries thought it in their schools.

National anxiety over the behaviour of the young outside the school gates is indisputable. The Prime Minister has placed it at the top of his priorities alongside global warming, international terrorism and the NHS. The dreadful litany of the anti-social behaviour of the young – binge drinking, vandalism, lethal driving, sexual irresponsibility and sometimes appalling violence – all adds to the outrage at a generation out of control, failed by the education system and neglected by its parents.

But is the picture really as grim as this? Or as simple? As far as the behaviour of the young in school is concerned was the golden age really so golden? And when exactly was it? Was it in the early years of the twentieth century when the Chairman of York City Council raged at the disgraceful behaviour of children who ruined a concert in a park, leading another councillor to declaim angrily: 'This is what we get from our Board School teaching' (*Yorkshire Evening Press* 04/07/05)? Was it a decade later, on the eve of the first world war, when the pupils of Ledbury Girls' School rioted after the appointment of a new headmistress? (Horn, 1985 p191). To the disgust of the girls, she had replaced their old head who was on strike with her colleagues. They chased her off the premises and then created mayhem in the school, overturning desks 'to a piano accompaniment' At least standards in music were satisfactory.

Did the golden age arrive with the end of the great war when the pupils of Graham Greene's father, the head of Berkhampstead School, determined to celebrate Armistice Day by throwing him in a nearby river? They arrived at the school gates in their hundreds, accompanied by a motley collection of townsfolk and drunken soldiery. Greene narrowly escaped and subsequently expelled 122 boys but later relented, sparing all except two who had planned to drown his much loved book collection alongside him (Sherry, 1989 p60).

S.F Hatton, watching a class in a London secondary school in 1931, seemed unaware of any golden age.

> Four lads were taking potshots, out of the window, with inkwells at passers by in the street... another group were playing cards... several were pushing desks around for fun and three or four were pretending to listen in the front row to the teacher declaiming, 'What is liberty?' (Pearson, 1983 p13)

Around this time Arthur Shipley, teaching in Sheffield, was moved suddenly to another school where his new headmaster greeted him, 'This is your class. The teacher's in hospital' – a pupil had attacked him (Cunningham and Gardner, 2004 p205).

If there was an era of improved behaviour amongst the young, perhaps it was in the fifteen years from the end of world war two to around 1960. It is plausible that the sense of social harmony created by that war and the respect felt by youngsters for the sacrifices made by the older generation ushered in a calmer, more disciplined age. As a result schools may have become more orderly institutions than before or since. But the evidence suggests that even if this were so, the extent of the change was not as marked as often thought.

The positive views of my *Saga* correspondents must be measured against the fact that most attended grammar schools or were in the top set of secondary moderns. They achieved well by the standards of the time and the correlation between poor behaviour and academic failure in schools is indisputable. Even so, a number of them described serious discipline problems. Whilst some maintain that bullying did not exist in schools then, others like Isabella Palmer in Sunderland testify that they were badly bullied. Rodney Minns wrote about his school, which '...was quite rough and whenever... a large group (was) congregating... either a fight was in progress or a boy was disrobing a girl. (Some) lessons were a joke and we (including the teacher) just fooled around all the time'.

Paul Brinlow's friends amused themselves 'shooting cigarettes out of each others' mouths with a slug gun'. A colleague of Ed Adams in Leeds 'could not maintain order at all and his class was conducted amidst a scene of continuous chaos', whilst Jill Berelson told of older boys occasionally 'reciprocating' against physical handling by staff.

The first section of Edward Blishen's description of teaching at a boys secondary modern at this time, *The Roaring Boys*, is revealingly subtitled 'war in the classroom'. After a pupil has attacked Blishen, another boy whispers to the teacher 'He's always hitting masters' (Blishen, 1955 p90). The academic, John Cornwell writes of coming home from his new secondary school 'uttering foul language... my clothes filthy from desperate playground fights' (Cornwell, 2006 p29). He had been expelled from his primary school for attacking a nun with a blackboard setsquare.

HMI reports from the time, whilst not reflecting as great disquiet about discipline as they did about academic standards, nonetheless reveal concern about behaviour. Significant discipline problems existed, for example, in a secondary modern in the rural North Riding and in a Bristol grammar school. In a Cumberland secondary modern there was said to be serious indiscipline, a lack of courtesy and widespread graffiti and vandalism in the girls' toilets. Three of seven science teachers at a Leeds girls grammar school were said to have 'serious disciplinary problems'.

References to problems in London secondaries were more frequent, with 'unruly behaviour' in one and 'outbursts of indiscipline against supply teachers' elsewhere. In one Middlesex secondary modern where poor behaviour in corridors and stairwells had spread to many classrooms, a shocked woman governor demanded to know whether corporal punishment was being used enough. 'Regularly' replied the senior inspector, 'the problem is one of lack of leadership by the staff'.

Meanwhile the press, although less strident than today's, was unhappy about the state of discipline in schools. 'Teenage thugs who flourish in Britain's blackboard jungle – where the masters live in fear', claimed a headline in the *Daily Mirror* in January 1956, whilst local papers told of 'Pupil who wanted to fight me' and "Blackboard jungle in local school' (Taylor, 1963 p165/6). In 1955 a New Zealand supply teacher wrote several articles for the *News Chronicle* about the horrors of working in London schools (Taylor, p37).

There was equal concern about the behaviour of the young outside school. A speaker at the Tory Conference in 1958 claimed

> There is a lack of parental control, interest or support. Young people are no longer frightened of the police: they sneer at them. Over the past twenty five years, we have cast aside the word discipline and are now suffering for it. (Pearson, 1983 p13)

The reference to 'the past twenty five years' is fascinating. The speaker apparently believed the rot had set in during the early 30s when the future heroes of the Battle of Britain or El Alamein were at school. He was not alone in his views. The president of the Methodist Conference spoke in 1956 of 'a generation growing up which fears neither God nor man and... neither believes in itself or anything else'. Eight years later, the *Readers Digest* was to write in terms which even a modern tabloid editor might hesitate to employ of a 'diseased harvest of anti-social youth' (Davis, 1990 pp149,155).

The belief that school discipline and juvenile behaviour have not simply worsened in the past half-century, but are of a wholly unprecedented order is due to ignorance of social history. Nowadays stories about a particularly vicious crime or incident of callous anti-social behaviour are frequently followed by editorials or letters which suggest that such actions were unknown in the past, not simply less common. This belief results from the low-key approach of the media at the time compared with the high profile reporting today.

Three dreadful juvenile crimes took place in the post-war period which, if they were to happen now, would monopolise the media for days and lead to anguished debate about the moral decline of youth. In one incident, with awful echoes of the James Bulger case, a 10 year-old boy in Glamorgan tied up a toddler, threw him in a river and calmly watched him drown. In the second, in Hull, five boys aged around 11 subjected a 9 year-old to a mock trial and then deliberately set fire to him. He survived, but only after his leg had been amputated, and suffered appalling injuries.

In the final, perhaps most extreme case, a group of boys at an approved school in Staffordshire had plotted to kill their headteacher. Somehow they obtained four rifles and live ammunition before searching for him. Although they failed to find him, they were challenged by another teacher whom they shot dead. Ten boys aged 15 were tried for murder. In court the ringleader said that he was sorry 'it was not the headteacher, but it was no good leaving him (the victim) alive after I had shot him once'. All three of these brutal acts took place within eighteen months of each other in 1947 and 1948 (*The Times*, 12/03/47, 12/07/47, 21/10/48).

Looked at from a modern perspective these cases had two unexpected features. In the Hull case, the sentence was astonishingly lenient. The culprits were put on probation and bound over to keep the peace in the sum of £5. The magistrate said he believed that the perpetrators had suffered enough from knowing what they had done and urged them to take chocolates and flowers to the injured boy in hospital. His mother, not surprisingly, declined the offered gifts. The outrage at such an outcome now can be imagined. In the Welsh case the solicitors representing the accused offered to find him a home and pay for his education if he were spared detention: a response which would cause apoplexy amongst tabloid editors today.

The near universal belief that today that we live in an age of unprecedented leniency is open to question. Lord Baden Powell wrote in 1933 that the rise in juvenile crime was 'a promising sign': cases of robbery with violence and 'smash and grabs' showed 'there was still some spirit of adventure' amongst the young (Pearson, 1983 p34).

The second unexpected feature of these crimes was the restrained press coverage. The Hull case was reported in the *Times* underneath a story about the winner of the terrier class at Crufts, whilst the Glamorgan murder appeared, ironically, below a report of the Princess Royal opening a child welfare centre. Although the school murder was the main story on the news page, it was not followed up afterwards, although a later official enquiry into the case was reported. None of the cases was mentioned in any editorial or reader's letter. The reaction in a popular paper, the *Daily Mirror*, was similar. It covered all three cases but led with none; there were no references in any editorial, columns or letters and no follow-up stories. Such a reaction is inconceivable today. And juvenile crime was by no means uncommon at the time. The Metropolitan Police Commissioner, Sir Harold Scott, claimed that there were over 160 gangs of young criminals operating in London 'some led by children as young as 10' who had stolen property worth millions of pounds (*Daily Mirror*, 11/07/47).

Other factors besides media coverage may influence our view of how well schools today manage discipline compared with in the past. The further we go back in time, the more the average age of secondary school children falls. Before 1973 no 16 year-olds, and before 1947 no 15 year-olds, were legally bound to be in school. Whilst class sizes were larger, the effect of the increase in the leaving age, which was obviously desirable, was to add enormously to the demands on teachers in recent years. The increased size and sexual maturity of modern pupils means that teachers today face the physical equivalents of adults a century before. Criticism of modern schools for sometimes failing to manage pupils successfully overlooks the fact that no teachers in the past faced a generation as streetwise, physically strong or sexually aware as today's. Pupils in the early part of the last century, like those who chased their head in Ledbury, would probably not intimidate teachers used to dealing with modern Year 11 pupils!

Additionally, although no national statistics were recorded for truancy until recently, there is evidence that absenteeism, especially amongst older, more challenging children, was higher in the past. The Newsom Report (Newsom, 1963 pp194-223) quoted a truancy figure of 17 per cent for the bottom quartile of secondary school children, an unauthorised absence figure of 4.25 per cent for all pupils, assuming that no child in the top three quartiles ever truanted! This is over four times the modern figure. Some of this truancy was doubtless due to responsible girls being kept at home for domestic tasks. Other children who truanted might have made life more difficult for staff had they attended. Today schools are under intense pressure to reduce absenteeism and disaffected children are more likely to be found in the classroom.

Equally, the emphasis on inclusion today means that it is rare to see children standing outside classrooms during lessons and certainly not in the numbers common in the past. One correspondent wrote how her husband was invariably sent out by his history teacher in the 50s, even before the lesson began. Within lessons the disengaged, the bored and the uncomprehending were more likely to be left to their own devices than in today's classroom. My A-level English teacher, Terry Green, described a history lesson on Napoleon's battles, given on teaching practice in the 50s. Whilst the boys thoroughly enjoyed the gory tales

> ...the girls found it a bore. They simple carried on knitting, smiling now and then at the males playing soldiers. They often knitted during my classes: even at that age they had the feminine dislike of wasting time which was how they thought of my lessons.

This is an amusing account by someone who was actually an inspirational teacher, but it does underline the pressure teachers are under today to involve the entire class throughout the lesson.

There is substantial evidence to show that despite increased demands on schools, the truth about behaviour is far from the picture of widespread mayhem painted at union conferences or in newspaper headlines. The Chief inspector's report for 2004-5 found that behaviour was unsatisfactory in only 1 per cent of primary schools and 7 per cent of secondary schools. It was good or excellent in 90 per cent of primary schools (satisfactory in 9%) and in 73 per cent of secondary schools (satisfactory in 20%). Those figures have improved for primary schools over the past five years, compared with the previous five, and remained the same for secondary schools. A survey of parents in 2005 showed that the proportion who believed that behaviour was bad in their child's school had actually halved in the previous three years (*TES*, 03/06/05). The positive response from those who speak from first-hand experience is marked.

The major Ofsted study, *Managing Challenging Behaviour*, published in 2005 confirms these views

> The behaviour of the very large majority of pupils and students remains satisfactory or better. Most schools are successful at... creating a climate in which learners feel valued, cared for and safe. (p4)

The report stresses that the most common form of poor behaviour is persistent, low- level disruption of lessons which wears staff down and interrupts learning. Extreme acts of violence remain rare and are committed by a tiny proportion of pupils.

None of this remotely vindicates the fevered headline of the *Daily Mail* in the same year, 'The Collapse of the Classroom'. But nor should those who are outside the classroom underestimate the effect on teachers and other pupils of that persistent, low-level disruption which may continue month after month. Teachers are certainly very anxious about the issue. A survey for Teachers' TV in 2005 by ICM revealed that about 60 per cent of respondents felt that there was 'a discipline crisis in our schools', although the use of the word 'our' may be revealing.

About 80 per cent thought the worst problems were the behaviour of one or two highly disruptive pupils in a typical class plus more widespread low-level disruption. Foul language and the threat of violence to teachers, despite the media obsession with these issues, hardly registered. Low-level disruption is confirmed as a serious issue in the survey although nothing like the exaggerated picture of constant chaos painted in Channel 4 *Dispatches* programmes and elsewhere. About half of all teachers report losing no teaching time at all, or under three minutes in an hour, through disruption or disciplinary issues. Another quarter cite between three and nine minutes and of the final quarter, who lose over nine minutes, around half say the time lost can be up to 15 minutes. That final figure is disturbing, although still lower than Lacey's assessment in the mid-60s that around a quarter of all teachers had 'chronic discipline problems' (Lacey, 1970 p170). Nor is it always clear how much time lost is due to misbehaviour or whether it is the normal result when any group of 30 or so people settle down to a new activity. Nevertheless, the picture painted is supported by my survey of over 100 primary and secondary teachers for this book, most quoting discipline problems as the aspect of teaching which had most deteriorated during their careers.

The Ofsted report on behaviour lists those factors which promote serious misbehaviour. Some, like family conflict, drug abuse and peer involvement in crime are often beyond the power of schools to influence. But others, like failure in basic literacy, poor leadership by heads and senior managers, lack of a sense of school community or of good links with parents, inappropriate curriculum or poor teaching have all been shown to affect behaviour negatively. These are areas which most schools are working hard to address, many with noteable success.

In truth, despite the serious effects of low-level interruptions in class and the bad behaviour of some individuals, thousands of urban schools in England are actually oases of calm compared with the streets and estates around them and are often the only stable part of the lives of many children. This view is supported by Peter Hyman (Hyman, 2005) and Fran Abrams (Abrams, 2005) who both spent lengthy periods observing classes in London comprehensives. Research by the OECD also suggests that UK pupils see their schools as more orderly than those elsewhere (PISA, 2000 interactive ST2616).

The vast majority of children behave just as well as their predecessors and do so without the threat of the severe punishments which were used to control pupils in the past. However there has been deterioration in the behaviour of the most difficult children. There is a greater gap now, than in the past, between the standard of behaviour of the well-behaved majority and the rest. Many children behave much better now than their equivalents in the past: for example the top sets in comprehensives are far less likely to indulge in the organised 'ragging' of weaker teachers which was common in grammar schools. Ian Anderson, founder of the 70s pop group Jethro Tull, said that his classes were 'mercilessly cruel' to such teachers. (TES 10/03/06) and C. Lacey described 'the tortured embarrassment' of a grammar school master followed home by his 'jeering, chanting' pupils (Lacey, 1970 p174).

The greatest anxiety of parents around behaviour today in schools concerns bullying. Bullying can lead to a dreadful sense of isolation, worthlessness and loss of confidence and in the worst cases to self-harm and even suicide. Most heads see the issue as of major importance and will spend hours, with senior colleagues and heads of year investigating allegations. Attitudes to bullying have changed considerably over recent years. Almost all schools take the issue very seriously now: most people would rightly be appalled by a head or teacher who described bullying as part of growing up, as happened sometimes in the past. The Children's Commissioner for England is mistaken when he says that schools are in denial over bullying. As Kenny Frederick, a headteacher in Tower Hamlets, points out 'Bullying is endemic in our society and such behaviour is learned at home and in the streets. Schools do a huge amount to tackle and identify it but get the blame in any event' (*TES*, 25/11/05).

But if the approach of schools has changed, so has the nature of bullying. It is more likely to be psychological than physical. Many of the most intractable bullying cases concern girls, often surrounding relationships within a group and typically involving the rejection of one or more individuals. Often the situation is dynamic, the victim one week being accused of bullying the next so cases become extremely convoluted. Just when it seemed that the facts have been established, an earlier, unreported incident will emerge throwing an entirely new light on the affair. And when, at long last, the matter appears to have been resolved in the best interests of the victim, the bullying ended and relationships restored, parents will arrive at the school gates with noisy demands for the expulsion of half the student body.

These complex cases have led to the so-called 'no-blame' approach, which is an unfortunate term. I believe that few would suggest using a 'no-blame' approach when the victim and bully (or bullies) are clearly identified and the facts are proven. I gave one girl who had bullied a classmate a final warning but she nonetheless attacked her victim in town one Saturday. The police were informed and I expelled the girl, despite the misgivings of education officers over an incident so separated from the school in time and distance. I argued that the attack would never have happened if the girls had not been pupils at the same school and that it only arose as a perpetuation of the bullying. The expulsion was upheld by the governors.

As with other forms of indiscipline and misbehaviour it is important to keep the extent of bullying in school in perspective, devastating though its effects can be. The PISA programme in 2000 asked 15 year-olds across the world about the problem. In the UK, 92 per cent of youngsters said that they had not been affected at all, or only slightly, by bullying and intimidation. Only 0.03 per cent said they had experienced 'a lot' of bullying. In other countries on average the picture was rather worse. Eighty three per cent of pupils had been affected slightly or not at all, and 0.78 per cent had experienced a lot of bullying (PISA, 2000 interactive SC19Q15). These figures for the whole country are similar to those collected via anonymous questionnaires locally which suggest that about 8 per cent of year 7 and 8 pupils had suffered some psychological or physical bullying.

A report that there had been 2700 cases of bullying reported in Sheffield in the previous year made headlines in the local press and on TV. (*Sheffield Star,* 17/10/06). This represented about 4 per cent of the school population of the city. Schools will rightly continue to make the combating of bullying an absolute priority. The evidence is that they are neither in denial nor failing.

There is a great deal of hypocrisy in society about bullying – and about children in general. Children learn to bully at home and in the street as well as at school, as Kenny Frederick noted, and they are also taught by the media and adult society in general. Programmes such as *The X factor* that humiliate the weak and the inadequate, the crowds outside the *Big Brother* house awaiting evictions with placards proclaiming 'Burn the pig', teach children how to bully.

The response of media executives is always that their output is only entertainment and the people involved are adults who understand what they are volunteering for. Yet most children who admit to bullying claim in their defence that the victim had acquiesced in what happened and that the whole thing was a joke. It was only entertainment after all.

The hypocrisy of many adults towards the young often beggars belief. It seems extraordinary that Channel 4 will employ hidden cameras to expose the scandal of swearing teenagers in schools whilst simultaneously paying huge sums to foul-mouthed celebrity chefs. The demonisation of the young seems a particularly unpleasant characteristic. Granted, the anti-social and selfish behaviour of the worst behaved youngsters is horrible. But as commentators as diverse as the Prince of Wales, David Cameron, the Archbishop of York and senior police officers like Commander Brian Paddick have pointed out recently, criticism is now so all-embracing as to include almost everyone between the ages of 8 to 24. In one local paper columnist Chris Titley wrote of youngsters at a local comprehensive school prize evening in terms sadly never found in the national press:

> Often, all we hear are complaints about the young, so how reassuring to see teenagers of intelligence, wit and charm... what a marvellous bunch they looked... celebrating their success in academic subjects, sport and music.

He quoted Commander Paddick: 'the vast majority of young people are decent, law-abiding citizens who want to do the right thing' (*Yorkshire Evening Press*, 01/12/05).

Sue Kirkham, President of the Association of School and College leaders, remarked,

> When Tony Blair talks about the respect agenda, shouldn't he be starting with adults... as school leaders we know that modelling good behaviour is one of the most effective ways to teach it. Where beyond the school gates can young people find these models... few will witness them in every day life. They are even less likely to see respectful and considerate behaviour on television screens, in magazines and newspapers. (*Leader*, February, 2006 p4)

To take Sue's question further, will youngsters find appropriate models amongst those premiership footballers who routinely cheat and abuse referees or those super models and pop stars who abuse drugs and trash hotels? What about business leaders who award themselves huge pay rises, well above the average of directors of similar European firms? And what of the role of newspaper editors, prepared to wreck the lives of anyone remotely regarded as a celebrity, however weak or troubled? How many politicians anywhere in the world provide a good model to the young?

Ofsted surveys suggest that most state schools not only challenge bullying and harassment and control behaviour well but also teach children the difference between right and wrong, encourage respect for the feelings and values of others, and promote good relationships. The charge that moral relativism holds sway in schools, with teachers unwilling to condemn poor behaviour or attitudes, runs counter to my entire experience and conflicts with the approach of hundreds of colleagues with whose views I am familiar.

The approach to these issues has changed and rightly so. The 'do as I say not what I do' style has gone forever, thank goodness. In 2003 a number of students left my school, without permission, to take part in demonstrations against the war in Iraq. Afterwards I met them and said that I understood the strength of their feelings and was pleased by their interest in a crucial political issue. I also pointed out that their action was wrong and had caused problems for the school and for me, not least over our legal responsibility for their safety and education. We had an good debate, in which several of them revealed a sharp awareness of the Iraq issue, and they agreed to restrict any protest to their own time in future.

10

The end of the first eleven:
myth and reality

In no area has criticism of state education been less justified than in the repeated claim that the last third of the twentieth century saw a tide of opposition to competitive sport sweep through state schools. Some have even
blamed sporting failings at international level on this wholly imaginary
phenomenon. This charge has been regularly levelled by opponents of our
schools without a shred of evidence being offered to support it.

In 1998, *The Times* said that the decline in competitive sport in state schools
over the previous ten years was the result of 'aggressive political correctness'
(04/05/98). Ferdinand Mount claimed six years later that '...educational re-
formers took the opportunity of the introduction of comprehensive education to imbue the new schools with a different ethos-one hostile to competitive sport' (Mount, 2004 p268).

Also in 2004, Dr Andrew Cunningham stated that '...for too long there has
been the damaging view amongst so-called experts that team sports are
somehow wrong' and went on to suggest that 'this lack of enthusiasm for
team sports in part of the maintained sector is reflected in the high proportion of privately educated players in the England cricket and rugby teams'
(*TES*, 15/10/04).

Even the euphoria over London's selection to host the 2012 Olympics could
not pass without an unpleasant jibe from Alyson Rudd, writing in *The Times*
'I expect schools to change, to allow in the competitive streak that they have
been trying to eradicate' (07/07/05). In August 2006 a spokesman for the
Campaign for Real Education claimed that 'there had in state education been
a general move towards removing competition for schools' (*Yorkshire Evening*

Press, 11/08/06) whilst a *Daily Mail* columnist later demanded that a future government should 'reintroduce competitive sport' (03/10/06).

The facts are entirely different. As early as 1987 the Conservative government commissioned an enquiry into the issue, headed by Elizabeth Murdoch. She found no evidence of 'any philosophy (in schools) that is against competition' and noted that 'allegations have been made that are without foundation'. (*The Times,* 04/05/87). Two years later *The Times* stated that only one of sixty education authorities controlled by the Labour party, Sheffield, opposed competitive games. Even this single example was not clear cut. The council PE adviser had said that although they believed that many primary children were too young for full-side team sports, 'it was not the authority's policy to discourage competition in schools' and 'there was no objection at all to team games in secondary schools' (18/11/89).

In 1991 Denis Howell, sports minister in the Labour governments of the 1970s and an ex-Football League referee, reacted angrily to comments by a Conservative MP in the Commons about the Inner London Education Authority. The MP had claimed that it was ILEA which had first introduced 'the absurd principle that competitive sports were injuring the growth of children'. Howell replied that he had personally investigated this matter in great detail and found there was no truth whatever in the allegation (Hansard, 21/11/91). ILEA itself launched its own independent enquiry into the issue, headed by a barrister, which found that only three primary schools, out of a total of 750 in the authority, were failing to encourage competitive sport!

In 2005, a survey in *Country Life* magazine of both state and independent schools found that over-competitive parents, especially in primary schools, were spoiling sports days by putting too much pressure on their children. The editor commented that '...some parents have a highly competitive attitude to life and are neurotic about their children succeeding at everything they attempt. It is spoiling the whole thing' (BBC news website 24/06/05). A headteacher banning sports days for this reason is not guilty of opposing competition.

In nearly 40 years of teaching, I didn't meet a single headteacher, teacher, governor, local authority inspector or officer who opposed competitive sport. Members of the council of the Association of School and College Leaders were asked about the issue. Not one of them had come across such views, let alone held them. Significantly, the most trenchant dismissal of the criticisms came from an independent school head on the council, Bernard Trafford of Wolverhampton Grammar School:

> I know of *no* maintained schools that do any of those iconic 'anti-standards' things that are so often demonised: and that includes all the schools in and around Wolverhampton that my school, for example, plays sport against.

One can only wonder at what the critics imagine actually happens in comprehensive schools. Do they really believe that Wayne Rooney, Kelly Holmes, Michael Vaughan or Andrew Flintoft were regularly harangued at assemblies and in changing rooms by their heads and PE teachers about the evils of competition?

Dig deeper and the arguments fall apart. Dr Andrew Cunningham claims that 'ideology' has resulted in the high proportion of privately educated players in the current England rugby and cricket teams. He conveniently ignores football, by far the most popular team game in state schools, whilst presumably by rugby he means rugby union. Neither soccer nor rugby league is noted for the large numbers of ex-independent school pupils in the national teams. Even his comments on cricket are debatable. Of the England team which regained the Ashes at the Oval in 2005, nine players had been to school in England: seven were educated in the state system, including the captain, vice-captain and man of the series.

The view that an ideologically driven decline in school sport has reduced our performance at international level can be as easily dismissed. If it is assumed that sportsmen and women before the mid-1970s were unlikely to have been influenced by politically correct views at school, whilst those competing since might have been, this has had no effect. There has been no overall decline in English or British performance in international sport in the later period.

For all the disappointment of the World Cup of 2006, England's place as defeated quarter finalists was typical of its performances in the competition since 1950, with the exceptions of the 1966 success which was won with home advantage and the semi-final place in 1990 in Italy. No modern England team has suffered a humiliation remotely like the thirteen goals conceded to Hungary in two games in 1953 and 1954. In the 1948 Olympic games Britain became the first host nation to finish outside the top ten in the final medals' table since the modern Olympic era began in 1896, and four years later in Helsinki we failed to win a single athletics gold.

The Ashes victory in 1953 is still remembered but other defeats in the postwar years by Australia, West Indies and even New Zealand are quietly forgotten. And the last thirty years have seen an enormous rise both in the standards of international sport and the numbers of countries participating. Whilst English soccer teams of the 50s and 60s faced strong competition from

Brazil, West Germany or Hungary, no Asian or African team posed any threat and the best days of French or Dutch football lay ahead.

Responding to Andrew Cunningham's article, Andrew Connell, who had run cricket teams in a comprehensive school, denied that the decline of the game was due to 'trendy anti-competitiveness', asserting that it was the result of financial constraints 'making it impossible to maintain pitches and replace expensive equipment' (*TES*, 12/11/04).

If there has been a decline in competitive sport, Andrew Connell is right in that it has nothing to do with ideology. The reasons are more complex and numerous, including the long-term effects of teacher industrial action in the 1980s. In addition, the pressure on teachers, who are not PE specialists, created by league tables and the national curriculum, means they must concentrate on their own subjects and this has reduced their participation in games. Just as important are changing social patterns such as the number of teenagers working after school and on Saturdays.

Yet despite such constraints, the range of extra-curricular sporting activities in state schools is far wider than in the past. At school in the 50s, we played soccer in the winter and cricket in the summer. Although we had an annual sports day, athletics featured little, whilst a campaign by sixth formers to introduce rugby was vigorously opposed by the PE department! In contrast to the limited range of sports available in the past, the mixed school where I was head offered soccer, rugby, hockey, netball, tennis, swimming, badminton, basketball, athletics and dance. Schools across the country, both primary and secondary, continue to play competitive fixtures against other schools in a range of sports. Sue Campbell, head of UK Sport, has pointed out that 80 per cent of schools currently run competitive sports days (*Daily Telegraph*, 19/09/06). If competitive sport really has disappeared from schools, how has the English Schools Football Association managed to sign up more than half of all the state schools in the country? What could be the purpose of so many schools joining something which they oppose on principle? In addition, many schools have introduced new sports, like Australian rules football at Carshalton Boys' School in Sutton. Others, like Hackney Free and Parochial School, have built climbing walls or introduced orienteering and mountain biking to offer fresh challenges.

Extra-curricular activities extend far beyond sport. The performing arts, clubs, excursions and residential trips have always been regarded as more integral to the British school system than in many countries. HMI reports from the 1950s and the recollections of those at school after the war suggest that the range of extra-curricular activities on offer then, including overseas trips, was surprisingly rich, given the financial constraints of the period and the difficulties of the time. However many people who have no direct contact with state schools believe that extra-curricular activities play no role at all in modern school life outside the independent sector.

There are no detailed comparative statistics on how this aspect of school life has changed over time, no equivalent of examination and test results to argue over. Nevertheless, evidence from the annual reports of Ofsted suggests that there has been no decline in extra-curricular opportunities, certainly in the last decade or so.

Commenting on the first four years of Ofsted inspections, the chief inspector noted in 1997 that 'extra-curricular provision in secondary schools has maintained its strength... and is good or better in four out of five schools' (Ofsted, 1997 p120). The report lists sport, art, theatre visits and field trips, orchestras, residential visits, community service, work with professional artists, musicians and dancers, and links with higher education. Detailed reference is also made to the growing trend for schools to use time outside the main school day to extend the curriculum through homework clubs, extra GCSEs or provision for gifted pupils.

Although the regular annual reports of chief inspectors have not covered extra-curricular opportunities in detail, the latest figures suggest no deterioration from the period 1993 to 1997. The chief inspector's report on the school year 2004-5 says that participation in sport is good or better in 89 per cent of schools, in the arts in 76 per cent and in other activities in 81 per cent. In 2005, as part of its preparation for extending the school day nationally, the government asked BMRB Social Research to analyse the extent of all current provision. They found that 99 per cent of secondary schools had supervised opportunities in sport, the arts, ICT and clubs and that 95 per cent had supervised homework and coursework clubs. Interestingly, 61 per cent of secondary schools had supervised activities before school. Although the figures for primary schools were somewhat lower, 87 per cent still offered after-school provision and 40 per cent before school activities. As these figures are so high, it is inconceivable that there has been any reduction in the opportunities available to children over the years. Despite the strength of extra-curricular life in many schools after the war, inspectors' reports and comments from correspondents suggest that there was a minority of schools, perhaps larger than today, where little happened after the final bell.

To gain a more detailed view of the position in individual schools, I looked at the most recent Ofsted reports of nine English secondary schools – one in each of the Ofsted regions. All had been inspected since 2003. The schools were in Dorset, Ealing, Hampshire, Kirklees, Leicester, Manchester, Norfolk, North Tyneside, and Staffordshire. Although it was a small sample, these schools were not unrepresentative in terms of overall judgements given by Ofsted. Two were described as 'very good', several as 'improving' or 'successful', one 'satisfactory' and one had been found inadequate and given notice to improve. Even in the good schools inspectors judged some features as unsatisfactory, including ICT in one school and provision for pupils with special education needs in another.

What is striking is that despite a mixed picture overall, the inspectors viewed extra-curricular provision very favourably in all nine schools. Comments on team sports, supposedly nearly extinct in the maintained sector include:

> 'school teams take part in many inter-school competitions and gain much success. Many students have represented the district and county... and some have gained international honours.' (Dorset school).

> '..pupils regularly take part in a good range of team sports and matches in local leagues.' (Kirklees school),

and

> 'Nearly a third of students are involved in extra sports activities.' (Manchester school).

In several schools inspectors commented on thriving Duke of Edinburgh Award schemes, some involving hundreds of pupils. In the arts, drama was described as 'thriving' in one school whilst another had an orchestra, bands, regular pupil performances and visits by English National Opera and Ballet Rambert. A third school had three large bands with 'a very good standard of performance achieved', and a fourth had 'a major high quality dramatic production each year which involves significant numbers of pupils as actors, musicians, designers and stage-hands'.

The schools ran many residential trips, including visits to France, Germany, Spain and China, as well as field trips and visits to outdoor pursuit centres.

Note that these schools were selected at random. Nothing was known of their extra-curriculum provision beforehand. A choice could have been made from dozens of secondary schools with extraordinarily rich and varied out-of-school activities, matching those of schools anywhere in the industrialised world.

Roger Pope, Head of Kingsbridge Community College in Devon, describes an activities week at his school. Some pupils were visiting Argentina, others a partner school in Bangkok, the band was performing in Austria, one group was walking in Spain, others camping in Cornwall and three groups were in France improving their language skills. He points out

> Teachers do not choose their job because they want to drill kids to get an extra percentage point in the next key stage test but because they want to make life better... Our school is not unique; all over the country staff are taking trips and they are heroes. Yet we do not know how many, because they are not seen as important enough for anyone to count. (*TES*, 21/07/06)

So far, this chapter has largely reflected a traditional view of extra-curricular provision in schools. But many schools are taking their responsibilities much further, with the introduction of a structured extension to the day which is referred to, especially in primary schools, as 'wrap-around care'. The DfES has suggested that many schools should open from 8.00 am to 6.00pm. The plan has met with criticism. Some schools are understandably concerned that even if fully funded, the development is more to do with childcare than education. Other critics see the long shadow of the nanny state in the proposal, arguing that responsibilities are being shifted from feckless or career-obsessed parents. Some wonder how young children, in particular, will cope with 10-hour stints in the same building.

Yet the concept of the extended school is not new. Cambridgeshire village colleges such as Sawston, the brainchild of Henry Morris, have been offering 'cradle to grave education' since the 1930s. Winifred Holtby School in Hull has up to 150 pupils attending school on Saturday who are provided with breakfast before classes start. If the finance, staffing, training and facilities are right, which is by no means certain of course, the prospects are exciting. It has apparently escaped the attention of some opponents of the scheme that a major attraction of independent schools for many parents is that they provide supervision and care outside traditional school hours. Are boarding schools not offering 'wrap-around care' *par excellence*?

Whilst the DfES places childcare at the centre of the plan, it also argues that activities need to be varied and interesting and that sport, the arts and ICT, key areas of existing extra-curricular programmes, should lie at their heart. It also points out that a pilot programme in 2004 found that, if properly funded, burdens on teachers were actually reduced through additional services to help with pupils' non-academic problems. Attendance, attainment and be-haviour all improved. Heads, teachers and governors will wait for funding and reserve their judgement but at best the policy could help to make a reality of the 'Every child matters' agenda with its stress on children's health, safety, happiness and achievement.

11

Schools for the twenty-first century

State schools are achieving more than schools in the past or schools in much of the developed world, despite facing considerable social and cultural challenges. With over 20,000 schools in the country serving vastly different communities, some will inevitably be less effective than others. The issue of how to improve schools has increasingly exercised educationalists and politicians across the world over the past twenty-five years. The solutions proposed often prove to be unsustainable over time or they fail to transfer successfully to other countries or cultures.

However, the last decade has seen growing consensus on the key reasons why some schools, both primary and secondary, are so successful, once differences in intake are allowed for. To explore the issue further, I visited several schools known to be very good, even outstanding. The number was kept small so that the reasons for their success could be considered in detail. A key aim of the visits was to decide whether the most important reasons behind the good performance of the schools were common to all or most of them.

The five schools looked at were:

Secondary	Primary
Broxbourne, Hertfordshire.	Maybury, Hull.
Kingsmeadow, Gateshead.	Holme on Spalding Moor, East Riding of Yorkshire.
Park High School, Harrow.	

Reviewing the evidence, it became clear that the reasons these schools did well were common to most. Many in education will not find the conclusions original: several of the factors have been identified by Ofsted or the National College of School Leadership as having substantial bearing on school improvement. However, I visited the schools with an open mind and tried to be influenced only by what I saw. The main characteristics of these schools are:

- strong, moral purpose and clear vision
- a warm, friendly and welcoming atmosphere
- an inclusive approach to all pupils
- continual emphasis on improving teaching and learning, supported by good use of data on pupils
- a self-critical approach, with good ideas shared amongst all staff
- strong emphasis on creativity
- varied programmes of well-run, extra-curricular activities
- attention to organisational details
- pupils having a real voice in the school
- shared leadership and responsibilities

Kingsmeadow is an 11-16 mixed comprehensive school on a sloping site overlooking the Tyne, in the Dunston area of Gateshead. It serves an area of high social deprivation with 40 per cent of its 1000 pupils entitled to free school meals – far higher than average. The percentages of adults in the catchment area with higher education or from higher social classes are both less than half the national average. It is a welcoming and friendly place which is wholly committed to the improvement of all its pupils under the leadership of its head, Simon Taylor. The school is determined to succeed with the toughest pupils. Inclusion is no cliché here.

Maxine Webb coordinates the behaviour improvement programme, working with a team which includes social workers and learning mentors. She is passionate about her role and believes the days of schools working in isolation on social problems are over. Maxine points out that targetting absence from school, where authorised or condoned absence is the biggest problem, has reduced crime in the area significantly. Exclusions from school had fallen by 2005 to less than a fifth of those in 2000. Maxine is also involved in developing the extended school concept. A nursery operates on site for ten hours a day, there is an adult education centre with opportunities for shared family learning, a 'well being' clinic and holiday activities for families. These services have been publicised on a school radio programme operated through a local radio station, helped by pupils from the school.

Alan Bradshaw, an assistant head, runs a learning support unit for pupils who are unable to cope, for whatever reason, with the normal classroom. One pupil had a broken leg, another suffered from ME whilst a third was an asylum seeker, recently arrived in the country from French-speaking Africa, with poor English. The atmosphere in the unit when I visited was calm and purposeful. Alan insists on a high standard of work and is adamant that the unit is neither a punishment nor a soft option. One girl who had become 'completely switched off from school' was fully engaged with work and starting to return successfully to normal lessons.

Meanwhile, Kingsmeadow's most challenging pupils are taught at Lobley Hill community centre, about a mile from the school, as part of an alternative curriculum programme. I met a group of students there, mainly boys from years 10 and 11. Most would probably have been removed from school permanently if the centre had not existed: one pupil had been excluded from three primary schools. The senior learning mentors who took me to the centre, Rob Self and Christine Byrne, were enthusiastic about the difference they were making to pupils' lives and proud to show the results to a visitor. As in the school-based unit, the centre is not simply there to contain the disaffected until they can leave school: there is a strong emphasis on teaching basic skills.

The pupils at the centre, many of whom have low literacy and numeracy levels, take achievement tests which stress grammar, spelling and punctuation and are also helped to develop employment skills through writing CVs and taking part in practice interviews. The centre staff obviously have a warm relationship with the pupils: 'They are like our mothers', said one boy, only half jokingly. The staff strive to develop team working and raise self-esteem.

The pupils had enjoyed preparing meals for visitors, including their own parents, the headteacher and a visiting delegation of Chinese educationalists. They ran a lunch club for elderly neighbours and several referred proudly to their parents' surprise at what they had achieved. Local police had run sessions for them on drug issues. A highlight of their time at the centre had been a week spent crewing a Dutch tall ship, which had helped them 'work closely as a group'. All were working towards the ASDAN qualification which combines improvement of basic skills with adventure and residential experience, community and volunteering activities.

For several pupils, the most striking boost to their confidence had been the opportunity to address a conference organised by the National Children's Bureau.

One boy, Rob, told the conference how he ended up on the alternative curriculum programme 'I have been taking medication now for two years. From my first day at Kingsmeadow I was in trouble, I would disrupt lessons, was always on report. My behaviour became worse and eventually I was kicked out of school'.

But instead of permanent exclusion, Rob moved on to the centre:

> I have been here from the beginning of year 10 and am now in year 11. My confidence has grown and I am very happy here. I have 100 per cent attendance and have passed my bronze and silver ASDAN awards and have just started my gold award. On Thursday, we do outdoor activities, canoeing, climbing and orienteering – I always try the activity and encourage year 10s to do the same. At first, I was embarrassed about my spelling and writing (but) now I work on my ASDAN not feeling embarrassed about asking for help.

Rob finished by saying that, as a result of working with the elderly at the lunch club, he wanted to work in a residential home.

Pete spoke of being excluded from three primary schools and how, then, he was 'lonely, sad and (I) thought I was thick'. He described how the alternative curriculum programme had changed him:

> At first we spent quite some time talking and getting to know each other. For me this was good because it gave me confidence and they listened to what I said. I don't feel scared if I can't do something because the group won't laugh at me.

He described the sense of achievement that came from helping run the lunch club, working on the Dutch ship and the improvement to his reading, writing and number. He has decided he wants to be a chef and ended: 'I never thought I would say this: learning can be fun. You don't have to sit in a classroom to learn things.'

But Kingswood is a true comprehensive and inclusion here means more than just improving the life chances of the most vulnerable, crucial as that task is. I met Lauren and Mark, two lively, intelligent and ambitious students now studying for A-levels. Both had been encouraged early on by the school to consider university: Lauren wants to read psychology and Mark, English. They remarked on the help and encouragement they had received:

> 'The teachers pushed us – put on after-school revision classes. Nothing would have been too much trouble for them'.

An unusual feature of the support was that some key revision sessions involved a residential stay in Richmond, North Yorkshire, normally associated with outdoor activities. They were enthusiastic about the extra-curricular programme, such as the opportunity to debate live issues in Gateshead Youth Council. These activities, in a school serving a deprived area, are surely an important reason for its success. Apart from the usual sports programme, field trips and visits, Kingsmeadow has strong links with Africa, organises visits to the crown court where pupils meet judges and has run a community radio service. The steel band has performed at Newcastle city hall whilst pupils also put on a production of *The Tempest* in cooperation with the Royal Shakespeare Company.

Another positive aspect of the school, noted by the pair, was the degree to which staff genuinely wanted to listen to the views of the pupils. When the pastoral system had undergone a full review, some students, including Lauren, had been invited to give their views to a staff meeting: 'I was amazed at how much the staff wanted to hear my opinion.'

Mark and Lauren had also been impressed by the school's approach to bullying. An effective 'buddy' or supportive friend scheme means not only that children have someone to turn to if distressed but crucially that the buddy would be encouraged to approach a teacher or other responsible adult on the victim's behalf, if they themselves were too scared or anxious to do so.

Christine Brennan, a senior member of staff, had been responsible for the new behaviour policy described by Lauren. First, she showed me a DVD of still photos she had made. All the photos were of people: they included children, teachers, mentors and administrative staff, caretakers and dinner ladies. Everyone was smiling, reflecting the sheer vitality and joy of the place. Rarely has the shared vision of a school been captured so simply, so completely. Christine explained how the new behaviour policy reflected the school's moral intent. It was less fussy than the older one, based on simple, key messages such as 'attend', 'aspire', 'commit', 'behave', and 'care'. Christine told me, 'I love working in this school. I feel it is an honour to be here.'

This determination and enthusiasm for improving the lives of children emerged again in a meeting with Joanne Ottey and Michelle Musgrove from the geography and history departments. Ideas poured out, as they described ways in which they were aiming to improve their pupils' performance. They were delighted with the success of the residential revision project described earlier. They spoke of helping pupils' thinking skills through mind mapping and other techniques, of changing the approach to classroom display, of targetting year 8 (often a time when standards fall back) or of wanting to help to teach years 5 and 6 in the primary schools. They stressed that successful techniques to raise boys' achievement work with girls as well. Above all, they focused on the importance of getting pupils to do the simple things well, of teaching how them to study and how to revise. The pupils wanted to succeed: they simply didn't know how. Joanne and Michelle are superb examples of how good teachers in successful schools constantly evaluate their work, re-think approaches and share ideas. They also gain enormous job satisfaction, and both stress that they would do no other job than teaching, however much they were offered.

Not that staff at Kingsmeadow are trendy idealists or unworldly 'do-gooders': far from it. They have no illusions about the task they face. The head, Simon Taylor, and Peter Laverick, his deputy, spoke to me of the extreme, sometimes bizarre behaviour of some pupils and of the sheer impossibility of supporting some families without the help of Maxine Webb's behaviour team. They re-cognise the real challenge of sustaining improvements in literacy and numeracy year after year now that the slack created by weak teaching in the past has been largely removed. Overall, they remain buoyant and optimistic, like all the people met at Kingsmeadow. They are currently planning major curriculum changes and are totally committed to 'youngsters leaving here feeling proud to have been at the school', a view shared by everyone I met there.

Broxbourne School in Hertfordshire is 260 miles from Kingsmeadow. It would be easy to write glibly of 'another world'. Certainly there are major differences. Broxbourne is in the London commuter belt, with many houses costing half a million pounds or more. The extent of social deprivation is far lower: the percentage of pupils on free school meals is around one tenth that of Kings-meadow. But references to 'leafy suburbs' would be too simplistic. Whilst un-employment in Broxbourne is low, much of the work force is in manual working-class jobs. The percentage of adults in the catchment area with higher education qualifications is below the national average and only half that of Hertfordshire as a whole.

The similarities between the two schools are striking. Martin Titchmarsh, the headteacher at Broxbourne is, like Simon Taylor, quietly reflective. Both have a clear vision of what they wish to achieve and are prepared to genuinely make use of the expertise of their colleagues, including the youngest, and offer them real autonomy.

The use of data on pupils and subjects at Broxbourne is exemplary. Jon Hampson, an assistant head, is determined that information about pupils will be of real use to teachers and is aware of the danger of staff today being drowned in data which is neither fully understood nor well used. Each department at Broxbourne gets a single sheet of paper summarising its performance at different key stages. In recent years, around 80 per cent of pupils have gained five or more higher grade GCSEs (87% in 2006) but there is no complacency. Senior staff have looked carefully at the remaining 20 per cent, looking for common factors and trying to identify pupils who are likely to under-achieve as early as possible. Remedial measures have been set up in a scheme called 'Every Child Succeeds'. This has included using sixth-formers as mentors and intensive sessions in areas such as coursework.

Deputy head Paula Humphreys, who is in charge of the curriculum, was keen to stress that despite its academic success and its middle-class image, the school is not a *de facto* grammar school. She spoke enthusiastically of curriculum changes like the introduction of BTEC courses which would allow a group of children to achieve who might only have gained the lowest grades at GCSE in the past. Paula was clear about the role of leadership in the school: 'It's about giving people responsibility, real autonomy, but then they are expected to deliver. There is general accountability, not specific'.

Stella Ingham, head of geography, had little doubt that school succeeded as an organisation by prioritising 'what is important, e.g. assessment for learning, which really benefits the pupils. It's important not to do gimmicks or keep re-inventing the wheel.'

Her previous school, which had failed an inspection, had had too much data and conflicting advice. She thought that Broxbourne succeeded, in part, due to its flexibility and pragmatism. Staff shared ideas, both within and between departments, and picked up only on what worked.

Helen Smith, an assistant headteacher, saw the school as a community where all are engaged in learning. She told me of the numbers of teachers doing master's degrees at Cambridge and of a group in which staff from different departments, including some of the youngest, shared practical ideas on how to help pupils. Helen concluded that at Broxbourne the staff felt really valued and wanted. The head had the confidence to reject some DfES initiatives and so staff were willing to really get behind those which were adopted.

Keith Parris, recently arrived at the school as deputy head, pointed out that the basic structures at Broxbourne were no different from those at most schools. It was successful because the ethos was strong and supportive, there were no mixed messages from staff to pupils, and parents were made to feel welcome and part of the school. The important elements were right, such as communication and transition from primary to secondary, particularly with regard to the curriculum. This can still be a weak link: although most secondary schools succeed with the social side of transition from primary, some are less successful on the curricular side. He described one initiative which brought together several of the school's priorities. Evening classes were being run in ICT, in which both year 7 pupils and their parents were invited to take part. Not surprisingly they were very popular.

Several themes, identified earlier as characteristic of good schools, emerged in conversation with Vicky Wells, an enthusiastic young art teacher. She had experienced shared leadership, running a training session for the entire staff on improving pupils' listening and comprehension skills. She spoke eagerly of the collective approach of the school. 'Everyone works together.... each year I feel I am pushed to achieve something.' She spoke about the social, as well as the academic value, of extra-curricular activities. House plays and competitions, not simply in the traditional sports but in areas like hairdressing, snooker or cooking, gave everyone a chance to compete.

The students I met, like so many of the young people I spoke to in the schools visited, were impressive – intelligent, vivacious and funny. They were keen to talk about the wealth of extra-curricular opportunities, such as sports trips to Canada, Holland, Barbados and Italy – paid for by fund-raising in school – and a sixth-form politics trip to New York. One described their relationship with staff as 'like friends': they were 'dedicated' to their students. All were appreciative of the high expectations of staff: two of the group had applied to study veterinary science at Cambridge. Many overseas educationalists would be baffled by the patronising and carping tone which characterises so much debate about education in this country, if they were to visit a school like Broxbourne.

Maybury primary school in east Hull has a long, flat, rather dreary frontage which overlooks a road to the docks. Happily, the drab buildings are soon to be replaced but the unprepossessing exterior belies a happy and vibrant school inside, with strong emphasis on both creativity and inculcating basic skills. A morning assembly is accompanied by the pleasant sound of the school brass and wind band. Helen Dent is responsible for the youngest children in the Foundation Unit and is clear about her priorities, stressing the need to develop children's speech and language, including the ability to listen. The children are taught to communicate through play: behavioural problems, she notes, are so often the result of frustration caused by poor language skills.

The programmes for parents currently being developed in the school are also important to Helen. They offer the chance to share ideas about bringing up children and to learn more about key areas such as literacy. She dismissed the idea that such classes are patronising or 'nannying', pointing out that many of the parents have good ideas to pass on and that this is an excellent way of involving them in school.

Claire Patton, the head, entered teaching late after several years in farming. She is passionate about the value of education and has the highest expectations of her pupils, in an area of severe deprivation. She is determined to raise levels of basic literacy and numeracy in the school and so far she and her staff seem to be succeeding. In 2003 the combined figure for the percentages of children reaching level 4 at KS2 in English, maths and science was 121; in 2006 it was 206. Claire believes that an excellent way to raise standards is through the use of themes arising from major school visits to the Moscow State Circus or to the Deep, the huge new aquarium in Hull. She is aware that some of her pupils hardly ever leave the estates where they live and so ensures that no child misses a visit for financial reasons.

All the staff referred to the real gains these visits had brought, not only in obviously creative subjects like art but also in literacy as children were encouraged to write, read and talk about the wonders they had encountered. Kate Holloway, a young newly qualified teacher with a science degree from Bristol University, values the creative work with her class. She also notes how much her pupils enjoy numeracy work such as the mental and oral starters with which she begins each lesson. Catherine Furness, in her second year of teaching, is delighted with the growth in out-of-school activities since she joined the staff. She runs a trampolining club, and this has helped her to get to know children from other classes. She told me how work on circus themes had benefitted her pupils' writing and awareness of phonics. Craig Williams, also in his second year in teaching, told me he 'loves being here'. His pupils, he notes, are enthused by the hands-on approach but he sees no conflict between basic and modern methods: 'you must be flexible'.

Craig thinks that the literacy and numeracy strategies work well because the activities are well-structured but not too drawn out. He believes that behaviour is improving in the school and that this is the result of staff working together on the issue. The importance of a shared approach to problems, based on a clear vision of the school's priorities for its pupils, emerges as a key reason for it succeeding in spite of local social problems.

From a distance Park High School Harrow looks like an underground station – so much so that you almost expect to see the familiar circle and horizontal line above the school entrance. Neighbouring houses lie unusually close to the school entrance. Not that this seems to concern families nearby, many of whom are anxious for their children to attend the Park High. The school has around 1000 pupils aged, unusually, from 12 – not 11 – to 16, although planning for the establishment of a sixth form was in progress when the visit took place. About half the pupils are of Asian origin and Tony Barnes, the head, said that about 40 languages are spoken in the school, although most pupils are fluent in English.

Park High excels in a number of areas which are significant in school improvement. The pupil voice is particularly strong. A large group of year 8 to 10 pupils (year 11 were doing exams) spoke with enthusiasm of the school committee (council) which meets every week, more frequently than in most schools. They had a confidence in the committee which is rarely found in schools: 'you can go up to a committee member and it will be taken up'. Ofsted agreed: 'the school respects the committee [who] take their responsibilities very seriously' The group had invited the catering manger to one of their meetings and quizzed him at length about school meals and the company background. Some members had taken part in borough-wide debates on issues such as identity cards. The pupil voice in schools often fails, not at the interface between pupil council and staff, but between representatives and other pupils. This is not the case here. Park High pupils were also impressed by the seriousness with which the school solicits their views regularly on 'what is going right and what is going wrong'.

Ofsted said that the pupils are 'polite and courteous' and that their 'behaviour is excellent. They could have added 'friendly and welcoming'. But it was also clear that relationships between different ethnic groups and with adults in the school are excellent. Inclusion, in this school also, is a reality on the ground. Like so many schools, Park High bears no resemblance to the 'caring and sharing' urban comprehensive of media fantasy where academic rigour and high standards are disregarded. Pupils said that they worked hard in all subjects, had lots of homework and, apart from normal parents' evenings, had progress review days twice a year.

Ofsted had reported that 'the school continues to develop innovative improvement programmes with students taking responsibility for their own learning.' Bob Bailey leads on the Building Learning Power project, a programme developed by Professor Guy Claxton of Bristol University. The approach is highly structured, an essential part is regular review and evaluation to ensure that the children really are learning effectively. Bob stressed that 'the kids are not expecting to be spoon-fed by the teacher any longer... they know what to do when they are stuck'. He noted how the programme has allowed the brightest children to fulfil their potential. He also feels that, for the first time in his career of fifteen years, he can talk to people outside education about what is happening in the classroom and share his enthusiasm with them.

Tony Barnes sees staff development as the key, not only to raising standards, but also to retaining teachers in the difficult London staffing market. He took the unusual step of beginning school late – at 10.30 am – every other Tuesday. The time is used for staff in-service training. The sessions are well planned, coordinated by Tony himself and led by school staff. They are highly practical and aimed at teaching and learning. Topics have included e-learning, pupil grouping and seating plans, building learning power and getting pupils to give constructive feedback on lessons and their own learning. Chris Scutt, a young teacher who co-ordinates e-learning, explained what the pupils do before 10.30 on the training mornings. They undertake on-line assignments in those subjects which lose time through the staff development programme. Those without access to computers at home come to school and work on school machines, supervised by teaching assistants. Chris stressed how important it was that the work set was challenging and followed up by staff. His message to colleagues was that, far from replacing the teacher, working on-line could significantly increase the amount of contact between teacher and pupil. A GCSE maths re-take course was now being taught entirely online and there had been a big improvement in pass rates.

Jo Lambert, another advanced skills teacher (AST), spoke of the '...lovely feeling of acceptability in the school of all races, religions, abilities and those with disabilities'. She recognises as did staff in all the schools visited that, however good relationships are, improving children's performance in classroom subjects especially in the core areas of English, maths and science must lie at the heart of school life. She spoke with real enthusiasm of assessment for learning – of giving pupils in English the opportunity to mark their own work and also look at that of others, and of getting them to isolate one issue and give immediate verbal feedback on it. She had been amazed at how sophisticated children had become in their comments. 'At first they only commented on each other's spelling and punctuation but now they are giving mature advice on how to improve writing skills.'

Violet Walker, an AST from the maths department, also sees real advantages in children working together. She completely rejects the idea that this method is 'trendy': 'It's how the majority of people work in everyday life'. She encourages pupils to share ideas, identify strategies and then evaluate them with others in the group.

This approach has not been at the expense of examination success, where pupils are tested as individuals. In 2005, 71 per cent gained five or more higher grades GCSEs and Ofsted concluded in 2006 that the school was 'very effective'.

Collaboration also plays an important part in Violet's efforts for the gifted and talented. She has worked closely with Harrow public school to put on study days for the brightest pupils on topics such as ecology and the 'world in vision': a theme based on the World Cup in 2006.

Towards the end of the visit a group of girls of different ethnic origins chatted in the entrance hall of Park High school. Around them were trophies for soccer and athletics and the national sportsmark award and superb pieces of mixed media artwork based on sea scenes. There were beautiful Indian silk paintings, close to a display about a year 10 trip geography trip to Swanage. Pupils had written glowing comments such as 'Swanage is an experience I will never forget.' Across the hall there were advertisements and a cast list for a production of 'Grease' which was to be performed in the last week of term. Ofsted were right: this is a highly effective school.

As I waited to see the head, Mark Alston, at Holme on Spalding Moor primary, children and staff were leaving the hall after assembly. Nearly every one smiled and said 'hello' as they passed. The school is housed in attractive Victorian buildings in this small East Riding market town. The distinguished old school building seemed an unlikely venue for the cutting edge technology children in the school were using. A group of able maths pupils were taking part in a six week live on-line course, Magic Maths, developed by the East Riding authority. They spoke to their teacher, Jan Stainforth, by audio-link. In fact, the children had switched on their computers and were busy on starter activities even before the teacher came on-line. The taught session began with the children manoeuvring cars and lorries into virtual parking spaces. The benefits to the understanding of space and length were clear. Later work involved the use of dice to help pupils appreciate relationships between numbers.

With any use of ICT it is crucial to ask what is gained which could not be achieved just as easily by traditional and perhaps cheaper methods. In this case, the work on spatial awareness was completed more accurately and quickly than if the children had been using model vehicles in a conventional setting. The teacher is also able to see the children's results at a glance and there is no problem about the teacher finding supplementary work for those who finish first. Feedback from the children is also immediate and there is a 'hands-up' facility in the programme for the children to use to call for the teacher's attention. Throughout the session, the children's attention never flickered from the task in hand: they were utterly absorbed.

Jan believes that it is important both to meet the children and to teach them face to face, sometimes alongside the class teacher. The advantages of making the best use of teacher expertise in small, rural schools in an area like east Yorkshire are obvious.

In Mark Alston's office at the top of a quaint spiral staircase he told me that he is prepared to invest significantly in ICT and sees major benefits for the children. It has for example boosted the number of level 5s in KS2 assessments (children with level 5 are very likely to go on to achieve good GCSE results at secondary school). Whilst more able children had been seen on the visit, Mark pointed out that computers are used just as often to help struggling pupils.

The similarities between all the schools visited are clear. None of the heads operate in the style of the dominant super head, supposedly parachuted into failing schools. All are quiet, thoughtful people, willing to share authority widely with colleagues and to listen seriously to what pupils and others have to say. They are self-critical and surprisingly open about what could be improved in their schools. All the schools were receptive to new ideas but also determined that any approach must be both sustainable and properly evaluated to ensure that it really worked for the pupils' benefit. None of the schools is obsessed with data and examination results but regard them as useful guides to how pupils are progressing. The staffs constantly seek to make learning more effective and to achieve this they all recognise the need to get the basics right. Not simply the core skills of literacy, numeracy and ICT but also order and discipline in the school and efficient organisation. The basics also include the right of children to have their creative abilities developed and to learn the key social skills of mutual respect – including self-respect – and tolerance. All the schools visited recognised their role as moral educators and saw extra-curricular opportunities as having a key part to play in this. They have all embraced the 'Every child matters' philosophy with its emphasis on the development of the whole child.

It would be easy to dismiss the schools described here as wholly untypical, as scattered oases in an arid desert. There are many state schools in England which are less effective, less orderly and where children are less well taught than in this small sample. But the schools visited are not unique. All are very good, some are excellent but there are thousands out there like them. As Philip Lane Clark, editor of the first edition of the *Good Schools Guide* in the early 1990s who visited schools right across Britain observed: 'In my own travels from Aberystwyth to Ingatestone and from Dundee to Devonport, I was enormously impressed by the quality of work done, often in very difficult circumstances' (Lane Clark, 2005 p6).

Many teachers and some parents and governors may have read this and wondered what the fuss is about, thinking perhaps, 'we have been doing that for years' Nevertheless, the totality of the good practice observed was impressive. And it is heartening to appreciate again, despite the constraints of the National Curriculum and the pressures of over-testing, just how creative, innovative and enthusiastic so many of our teachers are.

12

Conclusion: the media, education and the truth

The negative views of state schools held by many fly in the face of the evidence to the contrary. There was, as we've seen, no golden age in the post-war period with which schools today may be unfavourably contrasted. Although the late 1940s to the early 60s were a time of gradual improvement, all the contemporary evidence points to there being substantial under-achievement in secondary schools which was widely recognised at the time. The education of most children and especially those from the poorer half of the population was blighted, not improved, by selection and the 11+. English schools today compare better than usually appreciated with those abroad, particularly with countries which have similar socio-economic, cultural and demographic profiles to our own.

But above all there is a wealth of evidence from examination and test statistics, Ofsted reports, parental and pupils surveys, visits to schools and research material which shows that our children have never been better taught and have never reached educational standards as high as those of today. The average teacher plans better and has greater subject knowledge than those of the past. They share ideas and problems far more willingly than their predecessors did. It would be unthinkable today for a recently retired head to say with pride, as one did in the late 1970s, 'When my staff closed their classroom doors, they knew they were on their own.'

If this is the true picture, why are the media so negative? Might it be that as conscientious educators we are overly sensitive to what can seem a barrage of destructive criticism? To try to answer this, I examined 17 editions of the *Daily Mail* in February and May 2005, choosing the dates at random but avoiding the General Election period. I wanted to see how a typical paper of 'middle England' really treated state education on an everyday basis. The editions looked at included 25 substantial contributions on schools in news stories, features, columns and editorials. Of these, twenty were clearly negative, three neutral and only two positive. One of the positive contributions was a thoughtful and intelligent letter from Sarah Walton, a sixth former, attacking the concept of 'soft 'A-levels. In fairness to the *Mail*, it was the lead letter of the day and accompanied by the writer's photo.

The negative stories were characterised by a questionable use of statistics. On February 3 under the dramatic headline 'Collapse of the classroom', Sarah Harris wrote that the number of schools 'plagued by classroom hooligans has almost doubled'. Hidden two thirds of the way into the article was the actual increase from the 2004 annual report of Ofsted: from 6 per cent to 9 per cent. Although this increase was worrying, it was only half the 'doubling' of the original figure claimed. And both percentages were too small to sustain the lurid headline above the story. The following year the figures fell back again. On February 12 an editorial announced that a 'third of eleven year olds can't read or write properly'. This was the classic National Curriculum level 4 error discussed in chapter 6. The paper also said that 44,000 pupils left school with no GCSE passes: a typical misuse of an apparently impressively large figure taken out of context. Forty four thousand sounds a lot more than 2.4 per cent, the actual percentage of youngsters concerned. This figure has also been steadily declining, decade after decade.

On February 7, Melanie Philips claimed in her column that, according to Ofsted, '40 per cent of children are being denied a decent secondary education'. Yet only days earlier, Ofsted had published its annual report in which no such figure or any remotely like it appeared. HMCI had reported that 7 per cent of secondary schools and 4 per cent of primary schools that year were unsatisfactory – hardly 40 per cent.

The use made by most newspapers of the 2005 report was breathtakingly selective. They concentrated almost exclusively on the small increase in poor behaviour. Few readers would have ever imagined that the Chief Inspector, although not ignoring problems in the system, wrote the following:

> More and more young people are achieving better and better results. We can say with confidence that more is better.

> We have in England an improving system of education.

> Commentators are too often wont to describe the past against some mythical golden age. The facts tell a different story.

> As the performance of schools has improved over the past years, it is only right that we have higher expectations. The celebratory voices of young people are drowned out by the doomsayers shouting, 'It's not like the old days'. No it isn't; and thank goodness, too.

Philip Lane Clark, first editor of the *Good Schools Guide*, has an explanation for the negativity of the press: simply that the media is antagonistic towards any state run or state supervised organisation. 'It is almost impossible for the Post Office, NHS, railways or state schools to get anything other than a hostile press' (Lane Clark, 2005 p6). Journalist John Lloyd takes another angle. 'It is an assumption common to intellectuals and commentators of both right and left that the institutions of civil society are doing badly' (Lloyd, 2004 p23).

Peter Wilby, ex-editor of both the *Independent* and, like Lloyd, the *New Statesman*, points out that nearly all senior national newspaper journalists went to independent or grammar schools and

> ...have little grasp of why schools have changed from the traditional institutions they remember. Moreover, a high proportion live within a few square miles of each in north London, which hosts enclaves of exceptional deprivation... and affluence. This gives them a distorted view of what most comprehensives are like. (*TES*, 28/07/06)

Wilby is probably right, although this still does not explain the misuse of statistics, selective quotation and constant over-simplification of issues to the point where truth becomes hopelessly distorted. The media practice of continually describing teachers and schools as either 'trendy' or 'traditional' obscures the pragmatism common to nearly all. Ted Wragg, in characteristic style, reflected on a lesson taught to 7 year -olds

> I had told them things, which sounds traditional enough, but we had done a fair bit of group work so perhaps I am progressive. On the other hand, I had told some of them what to do so I must be a traditional progressive, apart from when they are allowed to discuss the task... then I am a progressive traditional. (*TES*, 2006 p6)

Wragg once pointed out how no national test or examination results would *ever* satisfy some papers. If pupils do well the tests are too easy, if poorly then schools have failed and if results are in the middle they indicate drab mediocrity. He would have loved to see a more mature debate about education which moves beyond a national obsession with the minutiae of test and examination results – something that many journalists seem unable to grasp. There is no conflict between challenging widespread misconceptions about examination results and maintaining that we test our children excessively and place too much reliance on the results.

It might be more sensible to begin by asking why the most successful school systems in the world are in countries like Finland, with fully comprehensive systems. And why those which have maintained selection, like Germany, have failed to eliminate under-achievement amongst poor and less able pupils. Isn't it time to move on from misinformed and tired arguments for a return to selective education?

And there remain so many real challenges for state schools, including:

- how we can engage families who are alienated from school, more fully in education
- how the numbers of children with problems in basic literacy and numeracy can be reduced still further
- how we can encourage greater numbers to continue with maths and science to the highest levels
- how we should engender a love of great music, art and literature – including Beethoven, Mozart, Shakespeare and Dickens as well as the best contemporary works – in children who are influenced by an all-powerful media obsessed with what is often drivel
- how schools can continue to help the young appreciate the wonder and beauty of the universe and develop their creative abilities
- how we can ensure that they grow up happily in a multicultural society, developing tolerance, understanding and respect
- how we should encourage the desire to serve others
- how we teach the most appropriate skills, knowledge and understanding to children who will still be working after 2050, and how best use can be made of new technologies to achieve this
- how we can offer time and space to those who need it for reflection, peace, thought or prayer in busy and crowded school days

Any teacher, any parent, any pupil will add their own priorities to an already formidable list. Yet any debate on these questions should, though avoiding complacency, recognise the progress already made on these and other challenges which schools meet every day. That acknowledgement – pride even – is missing in too much discussion of education.

To take a single example: how much appreciation was given to the enormous success of schools in multi-ethnic areas in maintaining calm and holding communities together in the face of dreadful events like 9/11, the London bombs or the disturbances in northern cities? Did anyone not directly involved in education notice – or even care? Colin Bell, head of South Leeds

High School, had started the difficult task of merging a largely white school and another with pupils of predominantly Asian origin in July 2005. A formidable enough task but then the London bombs exploded. One bomber had attended one of the original schools. Despite some problems caused by outsiders and quickly quelled, the amalgamation of the schools was successful. How many business leaders or journalists would have accepted such a challenge or succeeded had they done so?

Robert Maxwell was wrong. Headteachers, teachers and other staff in our schools are not failing. The task they take on is both supremely daunting and incredibly important. Only by recognising what they are achieving can we truly give them the support they deserve. I let others provide the conclusion to this book of affirmation:

> Education should give us inner resources and independence of thought.
> **Anne Atkins**

> [The purpose of education is]
> To discover and realise the genius in everyone
> To learn about the people in the world with whom you have to live and their history and culture
> To acquire the skills to do the work you want
> To build up your confidence
> To discover the danger of hate and the power of love.
> **Tony Benn**

> Every school can and should... encourage an interest in that search for meaning, purpose and value.
> **Cardinal Basil Hume**

> Good teachers are being educated as well as educating, leading by example and demonstrating intellectual and emotional curiosity. It's like getting to the shoulder of a hill and realising it's not the shoulder after all, yet having the second wind to drive on.
> **Florence Menzies**

> Education is to help young people become more humane ... when it comes to the defence of civilisation, our fortresses are our schools, our heroes are our teachers and our strongest weapon is education.
> **Gervase Phinn**

And finally,

> There is no higher calling. Without teachers, society would slide back into primitive squalor.
> **Ted Wragg**

References

Abrams, F (2005) Better behaved in *Prospect*, 117, December

Adams, R (2003) Response to 'Cautions on OECD's recent educational survey (PISA)' in *Oxford Review of Education* 29 (3)

Baker, M (2005) *Whose expectations?* BBC website (07/10/05)

Bantock, G (1963) *Education in an industrial society.* London: Faber

Barber, M (1996) *The learning game.* London: Victor Gollancz

BBC news website www.news.bbc.co.uk

BBC website www.bbc.co.uk

Benn,C and Chitty,C (1997) *Thirty Years On.* London: Penguin Books

Blanden, J *et al* (2005) *Intergenerational Mobility in Europe and North America.* London: Centre for Economic Performance and Sutton Trust

Blishen, E (1955) *The Roaring Boys.* London: Thames and Hudson

Boyson, R (1995) *Speaking my mind.* London: P. Owen

Brighouse, T (2006) *Essential pieces. The jigsaw of a successful school.* London: RM

Brown, M (1998) The tyranny of the international horse race in Slee, R *et al School effectiveness for whom?* London: Falmer

Coates,K and Silburn, R (1970) *Poverty: The forgotten Englishmen.* London: Penguin

Cockcroft, W (1982) *Mathematics counts* (the Cockcroft report) London: HMSO

Cornwell, J (2006) *Seminary boy.* London: Fourth Estate

Cox, B (1995) *On the battle for the English curriculum.* London: Hodder and Stoughton

Crowther, G (1959) 15-18 (The Crowther Report). London: HMSO

Cunningham, P and Gardner, P (2004) *Becoming teachers: texts and testimonies, 1907-1950.* London: Woburn Press

Davies, N (2000) *The school report.* London: Vintage

Davis, J (1990) *Youth and the condition of Britain: Images of adolescent conflict.* London: Athlone

DfES (2005) *Education as a Graduate Career.* London: www.dfes.gov.uk/research

Dobinson, C.H (1963) *Schooling 1963-1970.* London: George G.Harrap

Douglas, J.W.B (1964) *The home and the school: a study of ability in the primary school.* London: Macgibbon and Kee

Elliott, B.J (1975) The development of history teaching in England for pupils aged 11-18, 1918-1939. Unpublished Phd thesis, University of Sheffield

Galton, M (1995) *Crisis in the primary classroom.* London: David Fulton

Gill, R *et al* (2002) *Student achievement in England.* London: HMSO

Gipps, C (1993) Policy-making and the use and misuse of evidence in Chitty, C and Simon, B *Education answers back.* London: Lawrence and Wishart

Gorard, S (1997) *School choice in the established market.* Aldershot: Ashgate

Gorard, S (2000) *Education and social justice.* Cardiff: University of Wales Press

Gorard, S and Smith, E (2005) *Beyond the 'learning society': what we have learnt from widening participation research?* Paper to British Educational Research Association Annual Conference,Glamorgan

Gray, A (1981) *Lanark.* Edinburgh: Canongate

Gray, J (2000) Discussion in Goldstein, H. and Heath, A. *Educational standards.* Oxford: Oxford University Press

Hattersley, R (1983) *A Yorkshire boyhood.* Oxford: Oxford University Press

HMCI (1997-8 to 2004-5) *Annual Reports.* London: Ofsted

Horn, P (1985) *The Victorian and Edwardian schoolchild.* Gloucester: Sutton

Hyman, P (2005) *One out of ten.* London: Vintage

Jackson, B and Marsden, D (1966) *Education and the working class.* London: Penguin

Jesson, D (2006) Performance of pupils and schools in selective and non-selective local authorities in Hewlett M *et al Comprehensive education: evolution, achievements and new directions.* Northampton: University of Northampton

Jones, K (2003) *Education in Britain:1944 to the present.* Cambridge: Polity Press

Joint Matriculation Board (1954-61) *Annual reports, examiners reports and question papers*: GCE. Manchester

Lacey, C (1970) *Hightown Grammar.* Manchester: Manchester University Press

Lane Clark, P (2005) in *SHA Associate News*: winter edition

Lloyd, John (2004) *What the media is doing to our politics.* London: Constable

Martin, F (1954) Parents' preferences in secondary education in Glass D.V. *Social mobility in England.* London: Routledge, Keegan and Paul

Massey, A *et al* (2005) *Variations in writing in 16+ examinations between 1980 and 2004.* Cambridge: Cambridge Assessment

Massey, A (2005) Comparability of national tests over time: a project and its impact in *Research Matters*, September (I)

McGough, R (2005) *Said and done.* London: Century

McKibbin, R (1998) *Classes and Cultures: England 1919-51.* Oxford: Oxford University Press

Mount, F (2004) *Mind the gap.* London: Short Books

Ministry of Education (1954) *Early leaving.* London: HMSO

Ministry of Education (1957) *Standards in reading 1948-1956.* London: HMSO

Ministry of Education (1957-8) *Annual Report 1957.* Command Papers Vol. X

Ministry of Education (1960-1) *Annual Report 1960.* Command Papers Vol XIII

NA (followed by reference) National Archives

National Audit Office (2006) *Improving poorly performing schools in England.* London: HMSO

Naylor, R and Smith, J (2002) Schooling effects and subsequent university performance: evidence for the UK university population in *Warwick Economic Research Papers.* Warwick: University of Warwick

Newsom, J (1963) *Half our future* (Newsom Report). London: HMSO

OECD (2001) *Knowledge and skills for life: first results from the OECD programme for international student assessment* (PISA) 2000. Paris: OECD

OECD (2004) *Education at a glance.* Paris: OECD

OECD (2005) *Education at a glance.* Paris: OECD

Ofsted (1997) *Secondary education 1993-97.* London: Ofsted

Ofsted (2005) *Managing challenging behaviour.* London: Ofsted

Ofsted (2006) *Parents satisfaction with schools.* London: Ofsted

Parker, H (1974) *The view from the boys.* Newton Abbot: David and Charles

Pearson, G (1983) *Hooligan. A history of respectable fears.* London: MacMillan

Phillips, M (1996) *All must have prizes.* London: Little, Brown

PIRLS www.nfer.ac.uk/pims-data

PISA 2000 (2002) Interactive database: http://pisaweb.acer.edu/oecd.

Prais, S (2003) Cautions on OECD's recent educational survey (PISA) in *Oxford Review of Education,* 29 (2)

Putnam, R. D (2000) *Bowling alone.* New York: Touchstone

QCA. (2005) *Review of standards over time.* www.qca.org.uk

QCA. (2006) *QCA's Review of standards: description of programme.* www.qca.org.uk

Ridley, K et al (2005) *London Challenge: Survey of Pupils and Teachers.* London: NFER

Sage, L (2000) *Bad blood.* London: Fourth Estate.

Sandbrook, D (2005) *Never had it so good.* London: Little,Brown

SCAA (1996) *Standards in public examinations 1975-1995: a report on English, mathematics and chemistry examinations over time.* London: SCAA

Secondary School Examinations Council (1960) *Secondary school examinations other than GCE* (Beloe Report) London: HMSO

Sherry, N (1989) *The life of Graham Greene,* vol.I. London: Jonathan Cape

Smith, E. (2005) *Analysing under-achievement in schools.* London: Continuum

Sticht, T (2005) *Towards full functional illiteracy.* www.basic-skills.co.uk March '05

Supple, C (2003) *From Prejudice to Genocide: Learning about the Holocaust.* Stoke on Trent: Trentham Books

Taylor, W (1963) *The secondary modern school.* London: Faber and Faber

TES (2006) Ted Wragg: a tribute. London: *Times Educational Supplement*

TIMSS www.timss.bc.edu/index.html

Tymms, P et al (2005) *Standards in English schools: changes since 1997 and the impact of government initiatives and policies.* London: Sunday Times

Whitty, G (2006) Achievements and inclusion in comprehensive education in Hewlett M *et al Comprehensive education: evolution, achievements and new directions.* Northampton: University of Northampton

Wilkinson, R (2005) *The impact of inequality.* New York: The New Press

Wolf, A (2000) A comparative perspective in educational standards in Goldstein, H. and Heath, A (see Gray, J)

Woodhead, C (2002) *Class war.* London: Little, Brown

Wrigley, T (2003) *Schools of hope.* Stoke on Trent: Trentham Books

Zweig, F (1961) *The worker in the age of affluence.* London: Heinemann

Index